ELLIOT CLARK

EVANGELISM

AS

EXILES

LIFE ON
MISSION
AS STRANGERS
IN OUR OWN
LAND

TGC

"Few things are harder, in the time of our sojourn in this present age, than to see ourselves as we are, as pilgrims. But harder than that, it seems, is the challenge of carrying out our calling as bearers of the good news. We seem to want to embrace the world in all the ways we shouldn't, while avoiding engaging the world in all the ways we should. Elliot Clark offers us a vision of how we evangelize in an American context. His vision is drawn from his years of ministry overseas and a heart for the local church. May this book prompt us to live as exiles and evangelists, at the same time."

—**Russell Moore**, president of The Ethics & Religious Liberty Commission of the Southern Baptist Convention

"What a profound, important, and timely book Elliot Clark has given to God's exiled peoples! We all know the world has changed around us. And we realize our gospel proclamation needs to change as well. *Evangelism as Exiles* helps us make the necessary shifts. And it does so with humble grace and deep theological reflection. I'm very grateful for this book and the insights it delivers."

—**Randy Newman**, senior teaching fellow at the C. S. Lewis Institute and author of *Questioning Evangelism*

"Even as Christianity cedes its pride of place in North America, the sky isn't falling according to Elliot Clark. Having spent years outside the United States, Clark recognizes the hopefulness of exile for Christians. By God's grace, we can be rescued from our bigotries, our cowardice, even our moral laxities and delivered into greater boldness. I'm both chastened and compelled by Clark's powerful, poetic words—and inordinately hopeful that we will reclaim the radical mission of proclaiming the gospel of Jesus Christ."

—**Jen Pollock Michel**, author of *Surprised by Paradox* and *Keeping Place*

"A helpful, hopeful, and very practical treatise from Elliot Clark. *Evangelism as Exiles* offers a much-needed real world perspective: cultural hostility against Christianity—often seen as a purely negative force by Western believers—can actually energize and revitalize the church's evangelism."

—**K. A. Ellis**, director of the Center for the Study of the Bible and Ethnicity, Reformed Theological Seminary, Atlanta

"As sojourners and strangers in a secular age, the call to Christian witness is one that can feel daunting to many of us. But as Elliot Clark's wonderful new book demonstrates, the opportunity is not to be missed. If you want to be challenged and equipped for greater faithfulness in personal evangelism, this is a book you can't afford to ignore. Through keen theological insight and careful pastoral wisdom framed by his own experience, Clark's *Evangelism as Exiles* is a powerful reminder that times of greatest spiritual darkness are also those of greatest opportunity for the light of the good news of Jesus Christ to shine all the more brilliantly."

—**Matthew J. Hall**, dean of Boyce College and senior vice president of academic strategy at The Southern Baptist Theological Seminary

"Perhaps you have practically given up on personal evangelism—maybe because you've depended too much on the attractional model of evangelism or because you fear the social stigma of speaking the gospel of Christ boldly. For those of us who are overwhelmed by the mounting evangelistic task, *Evangelism as Exiles: Life on Mission as Strangers in Our Own Land* offers us the biblical help and doxological motivation to confidently initiate gospel conversations in a society that is becoming increasingly hostile towards Christianity. The author takes us back to an approach that we should've never left, and I feel confident that you will be, as I was, greatly profited by this book."

—**Mark Allen**, executive director of the Center for Apologetics and Cultural Engagement at Liberty University and professor of biblical and theological studies at the Rawlings School of Divinity

"Elliot Clark's perspective is desperately needed—it's grounded in Scripture and relevant for the context in which the American church finds herself. He clears up so many misconceptions about evangelism that I lost count. I'm praying this book and its influence reaches far and wide to a great and lasting effect."

—**Gloria Furman**, crosscultural worker and author of *Missional Motherhood*

"We are reminded in this challenging book that there is a cost to evangelism, that we are exiles and strangers, that we too often long for comfort and popularity instead of speaking up boldly as disciples of Christ. Clark's book is convicting, reminding us of our great responsibility to proclaim the good news about Jesus even in adverse circumstances."

—**Thomas R. Schreiner**, professor of New Testament interpretation and professor of biblical theology at The Southern Baptist Theological Seminary

"This book offers conviction and challenge we urgently need, in regard to evangelism. It asks believers in Christ to grasp hold of our identity as sojourners and exiles. It speaks from the ground of Scripture. And it lets us in to stories of witness and faith in parts of the world where Christians know hard exile and vibrant hope. It's a book that helps wake us up."

—**Kathleen Nielson**, speaker and author of *Women and God: Hard Questions, Beautiful Truth*

"Having lived a good portion of my life as a stranger in other lands, I identified with *Evangelism as Exiles*. Elliot Clark issues a clarion call to believers in America to realize the opportunity for evangelism in a society that is more and more similar to the society that faced the early church—and we know what happened then! It's good to be reminded that though society has changed, the power of the gospel has not. Use the wisdom in these pages to fuel your evangelism in the modern world."

—**Mack Stiles**, pastor of a church in Iraq and author of *Evangelism: How the Whole Church Speaks of Jesus* and *Marks of the Messenger: Knowing, Living and Speaking the Gospel*

CONTENTS

FOREWORD

A rising number of Christians in the West are coming to grips with the reality that the Judeo-Christian worldview no longer holds sway. Of course, we've always known that there are parts of the world where missionaries undertake their work in the teeth of opposition—opposition that is sometimes cultural, sometimes judicial. At home, however, we didn't deploy missionaries: we deployed pastors and evangelists. But as the folk song puts it, "The times they are a-changin'." In the Bible Belt, especially in the population that is 35 or older, it's still perfectly acceptable to be a nominal Christian: the subculture reinforces us as we lurk in our pious comfort zones. Elsewhere in the country, however, and just about everywhere for young people, nominal Christianity is becoming obsolete: it costs too much, with no real advantages. Decidedly non-Christian and anti-Christian agendas, riding the digital waves, increasingly prevail.

It turns out that's not entirely a bad thing. As the number of nominal Christians thins out, it's becoming a little clearer who is a Christian and who is not. Christians are encouraged *not* to be like the culture, but to be countercultural. Pastors and others enjoin us to be like the people the apostle Peter addresses: sojourners, aliens, exiles. Instead of whining and feeling sorry for ourselves because the culture is becoming unrecognizable, Christians should align their vision with that of the most mature first-century Christians. If opposition mounts to the place where it can be rightly called persecution, well, then we are called to follow the apostles, who "left the Sanhedrin, rejoicing because they had been counted worthy of suffering disgrace for the Name" (Acts 5:41). After all, hadn't the Master, only a short while earlier, told his followers that if people oppose Christ they will oppose Christians (John 15:18–25)? So stop living your life in fear, and wear the cultural dissonance as a badge of honor. Fear no one but God.

Elliot Clark takes the argument one step further. The shifts in our culture, he argues, ought to modify our expectations as to what evangelism is, as to what evangelists do. Many of us think of Billy Graham as the archetypal evangelist. He sometimes went abroad, but primarily he ministered *here*: he was *our* guy, and he was feted in many contexts, sometimes labeled "America's Pastor." Now, however, the changes in the culture mean that, just as Christians face skepticism and mild opprobrium, so do evangelists. As Christians in general are thought to be too exclusive and narrow in their claims, too right-wing and old fashioned in their moral perceptions, and too out-of-touch when it comes to the freedom our culture hungers for in the domain of personal identity, so Christian evangelists fall under the same condemnation. Christian evangelists are not being celebrated in dinner meetings with the local mayor, but are quietly engaging in a one-on-one Bible study with an unbeliever, meeting in a Starbucks.

In short, Clark asks, what does evangelism look like once we see ourselves as exiles and sojourners? Where can we find our cues and learn some lessons? Clark draws from his experience living and serving in a Central Asian country, a country that is overwhelmingly Muslim. The West still enjoys more freedoms than Christians in that country do, but the question to ask is obvious: What should we learn about evangelism when we see ourselves as exiles and sojourners?

In one extended introduction and six crisp chapters, Clark lays out the answer he learns from Scripture—Scripture that is read when one is living as a cultural and religious minority. The clichés of our faith take on new and life-changing significance: what it means to live with the hope of glory shaping our priorities, what it means to offer respect to all (whether Nero in the first century or an imam in ours), what it means to declare God's praise to the nations, and so forth. None of these priorities is unknown or new, but they are configured with great freshness in the context of living as exiles. Read with care: this book may change your views on evangelism.

D. A. Carson
President, The Gospel Coalition

INTRODUCTION

EMBRACING

EXILE

"TO THOSE WHO ARE ELECT
EXILES . . . ACCORDING TO THE
FOREKNOWLEDGE OF GOD."

—PETER THE APOSTLE (1 PET. 1:1-2)

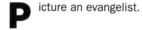 **P**icture an evangelist.

For many of us, our minds immediately scroll to the image
of someone like Billy Graham—a man, maybe dressed in a
suit and tie, speaking to a large audience and leading many
to Christ.

As such, we tend to envision evangelism as an activity—
more commonly a large event—that requires some measure
of power and influence. In communicating the gospel, one
must have a voice, a platform, and ideally a willing audience.
It's also why, to this day, we think the most effective
spokespeople for Christianity are celebrities, high-profile
athletes, or other people of significance. If they speak for
Jesus, the masses will listen.

But this isn't how it has always been. Not throughout history and certainly not in much of the world today.[1] And I suspect it will soon not be the case in the West either, as Christian power and influence fade into the cultural background in the span of our own lifetimes, as we lose our public and respected "voice" and perhaps even as we encounter persecution.

So we must learn what it means to do evangelism as exiles, as strangers and outcasts in our own land.

EMBRACING EXILE

I remember the first time it dawned on me that I wasn't a normal missionary. I was returning to visit the United States after serving in a Muslim-majority nation in Central Asia for a couple of years, and someone asked me a question I couldn't answer: "What does a normal day look like for you?"

I knew I couldn't point to any sort of regular ministry routine or schedule. Living in a Muslim country, I wasn't technically a missionary (not operating under a religious worker visa). I didn't have an office—not even a ministry budget. We didn't have facilities or a compound or a church building. We didn't run an English club, summer sports camp, or a VBS. We didn't operate a clinic or a non-governmental organization (NGOs weren't generally allowed in our country because of their association with mission activity). Any ministry we did was through relationships developed in our community

---

[1] Granted, we have examples from around the world today of large crusades. We can also find biblical examples of Peter speaking to thousands at Pentecost (Acts 2) and Paul reasoning with the crowds in Athens (Acts 17) or in Ephesus (Acts 19), but these were more often spontaneous and public gatherings, not exactly the same as planned events or crusades in the modern era.

or through my work, and we did it all out of our home—or meeting at a local café.

Honestly, there were days when I longed for the opportunity to operate as a "traditional" Christian minister. I thought it would all be simpler if I could only be known in the community as a missionary and have a visible platform for introducing people to Christ.

Looking back, what I now appreciate about that experience is that it forced me to approach evangelism and discipleship without the typical trappings of our Western ministry culture. It forced me to rely on the Spirit and the Word more than on evangelistic programs and events. It forced me to learn what it has meant for Christians in much of history to speak for Christ in their everyday lives, as sojourners and foreigners in their own land.

But embracing exile didn't come naturally to me. How exactly do you preach the gospel when both you and your message are unwelcome? How do you witness when you have neither a place nor a position? How do you practice evangelism as a stranger and outcast? Or, we might also ask, how did Jesus do it?

OUR EXILED KING

When Peter the apostle wrote his first letter to Christians living in Asia (not too far from my former home) he addressed them, curiously, as exiles. But these people were not literal exiles. They were not, as we might imagine them, like the desperate refugees and wayfaring immigrants flooding the West today from the war-torn Middle East or famine-stricken Africa.

This was long ago. Before Nero. Before Christianity became criminal in the Roman Empire. Before death sentences and political persecution. Instead, we might categorize the ridicule and social exclusion faced by most of those early believers as only soft persecution. Those Asian Christians lived with some measure of stability and comfort, yet they experienced repeated reviling from family members, neighbors, and coworkers. Friends openly mocked them for their faith, maligning them for their unwillingness to join in debauched parties and sexual escapades (4:4). "Christian" became the cultural byword for idiot or, if they had such a word, bigot.

When we read Peter, we might be surprised to see that he labeled such inconveniences and harassments as "fiery trials," even including in his definition of Christian exile the everyday challenge of having an unbelieving spouse and an unjust master. That's what suffering looked like for them. And, from such a perspective, it doesn't take much imagination to see how their situation mirrors our own.

However, Peter was most concerned with demonstrating how their circumstances reflected the life and afflictions of Christ. In the opening of his epistle, Peter tipped his hand to a theme he would develop throughout his correspondence: when the church is ostracized and suffering, we're following in the footsteps of Jesus. We're joining our King in exile.

In his greeting, Peter addresses these Asian believers as those who were elect according to the foreknowledge of God. Now, much has been debated about what exactly such foreknowledge implies, especially how God's knowledge of the future relates to our election. But that isn't our focus—

nor do I think it was necessarily Peter's.

Rather, Peter's aim was to highlight the overlapping realities of their experience with the Savior's. Jesus, too, was elect. He was chosen by God and precious (2:4). In fact, however we understand God's foreknowledge, we should take into account that Jesus himself was *foreknown* before the foundation of the world (1:20). In starting his letter with God's similar election and foreknowledge of his recipients, Peter showed their solidarity with Christ, who was himself foreknown and chosen by God.

But Jesus wasn't merely God's elect. He lived in the world as an exile. The stone God chose was rejected by men, becoming to them a rock of stumbling and offense (2:8). To paraphrase the words of John, Jesus came to his own people, but even they didn't want anything to do with him. And as we'll see in chapter 6 on hospitality, Jesus wasn't only rejected by the Jewish religious leaders of his day; even his own family opposed him. Foxes and birds had more of a home in this world than the Son of Man did.

Over and over in his letter, Peter compared the identity and experience of his Asian readers to that of the exiled Christ. They too were chosen stones.[2] They too were experiencing rejection and exclusion. Like Christ, they suffered for doing good deeds (2:21). In such cases, Peter challenged them with Jesus's example of entrusting himself to a faithful Father who judges rightly (2:23), an example they were expected to imitate in the midst of their own unjust suffering

---

2 A metaphor that should catch our attention coming from Peter who, as "the Rock," had already connected his identity and experience to Christ's.

(4:19). Because, as Peter explicitly stated, they were sharing in Christ's afflictions.

Now, we might wonder, if this is what union with Christ means for the believer, why would anyone sign up for such a life? Where's the dignity and privilege in being chosen by God if that same calling destines you to a life of shame and ostracism in the world? Why would anyone want to be associated with this Jesus? Then again, what did we Christians expect when we chose to follow a King on death row?

But here Peter answered with the New Testament's other-worldly and upside-down perspective. When we realize we're foreknown like Jesus, when we realize our sufferings are like his, and when we realize Jesus's rejection and his cross weren't a mistaken dead end but the foreordained onramp to resurrection and glory, then our faith in God explodes with the hope of our own future glory (1:21). The logic of the apostles is simple: If we share now in Christ's sufferings, then we will share in his glory. This is the ground of Christian joy. A *living* hope. In a world of seemingly unending shame, opposition, struggle, weakness, affliction, and persecution, the certainty of future glory is the unstoppable heartbeat of our enduring hope—and it will be our topic for chapter 1.

LEARNING IN EXILE

This is a book about evangelism. Such a book will inevitably talk about *what* the gospel is and *why* we preach it to others. However, this book will primarily address *how* we live on mission *when* we're strangers and sojourners in our own land. It's about how we present the gospel and represent Christ when we lose our positions of cultural power and influence, when the world has pushed us to the margins, when those around us oppose the message we're called to proclaim. It's about how we live on mission when we're exiles in our own land: in our workplace, our neighborhood, and even in our own homes.

As we start this journey—learning what evangelism can look like in the post-Christian West—we'll take as our guide Peter's letter to the exiled church in first-century Asia. I will also draw from my experience and perspective from years of ministry as an unwelcome minority in the most unreached nation in the world. But the lessons don't end there. Because as I've returned to my home country—a country I almost don't recognize for its new laws and new loves—I've also returned to a church environment that is deeply concerning.

So often now American evangelicals are despondent and hopeless, specifically in light of our fading cultural power and social influence. Our knee-jerk reaction is to bemoan what is lost, to throw up our arms and call foul. As the ground erodes beneath our feet, we tend to fight for our rights in the public square and slam our opponents on social media. We're fearful about our future. Yet fear of the future isn't necessarily the problem. We actually don't seem fearful enough, not nearly as exasperated or concerned about the certain and dreadful end of our unbelieving neighbors as we should be.

More and more I see Christians incensed when the world mocks us and our faith. But we seem to have no trouble disparaging others with whom we disagree, whether it's for their position on the environment or economics, guns or gays. Meanwhile, we unnecessarily disenfranchise unbelievers by becoming ardent apologists for relatively unimportant opinions, such as our preferred diet or sports team. But, at the same time, we somehow lack an authoritative voice on far weightier matters. Few of us would ever risk offending someone by actually proclaiming the good news of Christ. Instead, we'll only passively or reluctantly share the gospel provided someone else is inclined to listen.

We stand opposed to so much of what we dislike in the world, but then we live much like the world. Our churches mimic the value system of corporate America, promoting our professional ministries with the tools of marketing and amusing ourselves with endless entertainment. Then we're surprised when the world sees us as phony. So many of us are in love with this present world, yet it seems we'd rather keep the world—or, more accurately, its sinners—at much more than arm's length. Far too often we're a happy and hope-filled people as long as our churches are prospering, as long as we have a seat at the cultural and political table. But it's highly unlikely we'll invite the world—other races and creeds and lifestyles—around our own kitchen table. We're of the world but somehow not in it.

So we must repent. We must learn and apply the proper dispositions of a church on mission, living as strangers in our own land. While these lessons are found throughout Scripture, we encounter them most clearly in 1 Peter, a letter of increasing relevance for our day and time. These lessons are by no means exhaustive, but they are essential for any church in exile—especially so for us. Because these biblical characteristics are the ones that seem so glaringly absent in the American church today.

In the chapters that follow we'll consider six essential qualities of a Christian exile on mission. With the help of God's Spirit, such believers will be simultaneously (1) hope-filled yet (2) fearful. They will be (3) humble and respectful, yet speak the gospel with (4) authority. They will live (5) a holy life, separate from the world, yet be incredibly (6) welcoming and loving in it. While these three pairs of characteristics appear at first glance to be contradictory, they are in fact complementary and necessary for our evangelism as exiles.

YOU'RE NOT ALONE

We all know a seismic cultural shift is taking place in our land. The social pressures crashing against Christians and Christianity are on the rise and aren't likely to recede for some time. The West is fast becoming post-Christian, post-truth, and perhaps even post-tolerant. Our exile and persecution doesn't seem any longer to be a question of *if* or even *when*, but *how far*. How far will we slide? How much will we lose? How long will it last? And while those are all reasonable questions, the more pressing and biblical question is this: *How* will the church respond?

When you're a stranger, when you're on the outside looking in, you think what you're experiencing is abnormal. That you yourself are strange. But one of the essential lessons of 1 Peter is that this suffering and social exclusion is actually the most normal thing in all the world (4:12). It was normal for Jesus. It's common for our brothers and sisters around the world today. It has even been the norm for our African American brothers and sisters *in the United States* for centuries.

INTRODUCTION

For many in the African American community, suffering and exile aren't distant or abstract concepts. These are lessons they already know; as such, we have much to learn from them. In fact, I've found that if you read old Negro spirituals, you'll quickly discover many of the themes outlined in 1 Peter (and this book).

You'll easily notice their overwhelming joy and hope of glory. You'll see repeated announcements of fearful judgment. You'll read lines about respect and hard-working humility— profound in light of their many unjust masters. If you listen carefully, you'll also hear a powerful authority and conviction in their voices. You'll recognize them singing about "holy livin'" and most certainly their home in heaven.[3]

So, at the outset of this book, I want to acknowledge that while my primary experience of being a stranger and outcast occurred *outside* my homeland, and while those experiences will shape much of what is in this book, we should recognize that many of our American brothers and sisters have already lived through social exclusion and oppression *within* this country. For them, doing evangelism as exiles isn't a new subject.

I don't write that to shame those of us who are white and Western, those of us who are privileged with a history of relative ease. I write it to emphasize that we're not alone in this journey. You're not alone.

---

3 I should emphasize that I don't share this as one who has first-hand knowledge of the African American experience but as one who has observed these qualities in the beautiful lyrics of Negro spirituals. For one historian's perspective on how the Bible informed and inspired their worship, including how it specifically shaped their understanding of exile, see Allen Dwight Callahan, *The Talking Book: African Americans and the Bible* (New Haven, CT: Yale, 2006).

When Muslim-background individuals would finally confess faith in Christ in our former home, one of the first things I'd do is encourage them with the broader, worldwide body of Christ. They weren't alone. There were other believers in their city (I had to say this because I rarely met a Muslim who personally knew a single Christian). There were even other churches in their country. There were followers of Christ all around the world praying for them (this was true because of our faithful prayer partners). If you're a solitary believer stepping out on your own and away from all you've ever known, it's important to understand you have a grand, global family.

So too, as you walk the lonely dirt road into a shameful exile, away from what you've known in a sheltered American past, you're not alone. In fact, you're not even excluded. Just the opposite. You're being *included* into God's global family. You're joining Christ outside the camp (Heb. 13:13), bearing the shame and reproach he bore. But insofar as you share in his sufferings, you'll also partake in his glory. This is the solid basis of our living hope, a hope to which we now turn.

CHAPTER 1

THE
HOPE OF
GLORY

"BUT IN YOUR HEARTS HONOR CHRIST THE LORD AS HOLY, ALWAYS BEING PREPARED TO MAKE A DEFENSE TO ANYONE WHO ASKS YOU FOR A REASON FOR THE HOPE THAT IS IN YOU; YET DO IT WITH GENTLENESS AND RESPECT."

—PETER THE APOSTLE (1 PET. 3:15)

Our family's apartment building sat at the edge of a small city huddled on the skirts of a rolling Central Asian mountain range. On any given evening, from our third-floor kitchen window we could watch the orange sun plunge behind the ridgeline and spill pinks and purples all over the surrounding plateau. Turning to the southeast, half a mile up the hillside we could also see the last rays of sun glinting off the metal roofs from the nearby village. From there herdsmen would rise early each morning to lead goats and cattle out to pasture just beyond our gravel lot and across the bald steppe.

One afternoon, as my wife was working in the kitchen, I heard a sudden and sharp gasp. Then, without hesitation, she cried out for me to come. I immediately hurried to her side, assuming she was hurt. But there, from our kitchen window,

I found her staring out toward the opposite hill between our home and the village. I followed her sightline to the silhouette of our 11-year-old son standing on a mound of dirt more than a hundred yards away. Across from him was a group of boys, a village troupe we both easily recognized, a gang known by kids in our neighborhood as the "Rough Uncles."

As we squinted into the distance, our eyes locked onto the boy closest to our son. From his body language, we could sense this was a confrontation. In the village boy's hand was a large rock about the size of a football. We both watched, in stunned silence, as he cocked his arm and raised the stone in anger over our son. I froze.

For that brief moment we felt helpless and hopeless as parents, unsure of what to do and completely unable to rescue our son. Looking back, I realize I could have thrown open the window and yelled at the village boys. Or I could have raced down the stairs and outside to come to my son's aid. But would that have helped? Or made things worse? It all happened so fast—or maybe I was too slow.

But before we could muster any semblance of a response, the situation was somehow defused. The boy lowered the rock, and our son came hurrying back to the house, his face mixed with concern, shame, and uncertainty. As soon as he walked in the door, we embraced him and asked what had happened.

He told us the Rough Uncles had come upon him without warning (neighborhood kids usually avoided any contact with them). The group knew he was a foreigner and thus presumed he was a Christian. They asked if he believed Jesus is God's

Son who died on the cross. When our son answered in the affirmative, the boys were incensed and threatened him with stoning.

My wife, who by this time was almost beside herself, then asked, "So what did you do?" To which he responded, "I told them I wasn't afraid of them. I told them they could kill me, but that didn't matter, because I would just end up in heaven."

HOPE IN FUTURE GLORY

The indestructible future glory of Christians dominates the short epistle of 1 Peter. Writing to a group of believers in a world swirling with trials—opposition and rejection, sneers and put-downs, shaming and reviling—Peter's primary goal seems to have been encouraging his readers with the stable and assured future awaiting them at the revelation of Christ. So into their fiery crucible of suffering he injected a surprising word—a word of hope.

After acknowledging their status as elect exiles, Peter joyfully opens his letter with praise to God for their new birth by his mercy, a new beginning in life that leads to a living hope. But such hope isn't based in this life. It's a hope settled on the certainty of the life to come through Jesus's resurrection.

Peter then proceeds to dig deeper into this reality by revealing the Christian foundations that undergird such resurrection hope. As we've already noted, despite being foreknown by God, Jesus endured incredible injustice and suffering. As we know, he even walked the exile road all the way to execution. But that's not the end of his story or ours; God raised him from the dead and gave him glory *so that* our faith and hope would be in God (1:21).

We must linger here. Peter's logic invites our meditation. In Jesus's death and resurrection we find an unanticipated motive in the mind of God: the Father raised him and gave him glory *in order that* we might hope in God. Not just hope that our story's hero made it—that he's no longer dead. Not just hope that Jesus's kingdom would survive a lethal blow. But a living hope in our heavenly Father that he'll likewise raise and exalt us.

Peter wanted his readers to understand that God glorified the Son in order to give us, his children, hope for our own exile. Because when we consider all the trials Jesus faced, and when we see how they intersect with our own suffering and social exclusion, we realize we've yet to reach the end of our own story. Just as we've been united to Christ in his suffering and death, we'll be united with him in resurrection *and* glory.

Does that seem too good to be true? Does it seem impossible (or even unjust) that God would give us glory with Christ? Yet that's exactly what Peter said is going to happen in the age to come, and it's the source of overwhelming joy that led him to give praise to God amid suffering. "In this," he wrote, "you rejoice" (1:6). You rejoice because you realize earthly struggles pale in comparison to the glory and honor that will be yours when Christ returns.

Here's a truth we don't contemplate nearly enough in our prosperous Western context. When God set out to save us in his divine foreknowledge, he didn't merely devise a plan to remove our guilt and forgive our sin. He didn't merely provide a way to give us the perfect righteousness of his Son. He also didn't stop when he supplied us his Spirit to seal, guide, and sanctify us. No, his foresight and predetermined plan from the beginning was to lead us—you and me—out of our shame and all the way to glory.

Now, when some of us read "glory" we automatically equate it with a place. Over time, glory has become a synonym for heaven, but there is much more to its meaning. Peter wrote of our future hope more in terms of an experiential inheritance, a reward with social and even emotional dimensions. He included in that definition the tangible reception of praise and glory and honor *by us* at the revelation of Christ (1:7).

This is so astonishing it almost sounds blasphemous. If it wasn't in the Bible, we'd never believe it. But God has called us to share in Christ's inheritance and glory. To Christians suffering the pain of social exclusion, Peter asserted that God's plan for their lives wouldn't be complete until he had given them praise and honor *with Christ* at his return. So if you suffer now with Christ, rejoice! Rejoice because you'll also share in his glory.

Could there be a more unexpected promise in all of Scripture? But don't be mistaken. This isn't hyperbole. This isn't isolated conjecture. This isn't Peter being nice and trying to bandage our wounded hearts. This is the clear and repeated message of the New Testament.[4]

The apostle Paul says that if we suffer with Christ we will

---

4 For more verses on this topic than are mentioned in this chapter, see also Matt. 5:11; Rom. 2:7, 10, 29; 8:17; 1 Cor. 4:5; 2 Cor. 4:17.

reign with Christ (2 Tim. 2:12). In fact, he calculates that the suffering we endure (and Paul endured incredible affliction) can't even be compared to the glory that is to come for all of us (Rom. 8:18). Reflecting on our great salvation, Paul lays out the blueprint of God's redemption plan: he foreknew and predestined us; he called and justified us; he sanctified us and, as if that wasn't enough, he will glorify us (Rom. 8:29–30).

Christian, you know God loves you and has sent his Son to save you from your sin. You also likely know your great purpose in life is to glorify God for that salvation. But did you know God's grand salvation plan is to glorify you? This is what Paul calls our "hope of glory" (Col. 1:27). Peter concludes his letter by reminding his readers that they have been called to eternal, undiminishing glory (1 Pet. 5:10). One day, at the proper time, God will exalt us *along with Christ* (5:6).

When we face relational suffering and social exile, this hope-filled eternal outlook is what we most need. That hope, as our son expressed it, is a hope of heaven. Yet it's so much more. Peter wanted us to know that even though we face shame and scandal in this world, God's plan is to grace us with his honor (2:7).

SHAME SILENCES OUR WITNESS

So, you might be wondering, what does all this have to do with evangelism? How does a hope of future honor and glory change the way we preach the gospel?

We need to hear and believe the promise of our future

exaltation in order to overcome the threat of shame and disgrace that would silence our witness. The dominant reason for our lack of evangelism in America isn't the fear of death. We aren't in danger of being imprisoned or tortured. Rather, we're just beginning to face, like the recipients of 1 Peter, soft persecution. We face being ignored or excluded. We face ridicule or reviling. If we open our mouths with the gospel, we run the risk of others thinking we're closed-minded or unloving. And, at least in my own life, the mere potential for such shame, the possibility of being made an outsider, hinders me from practicing bold evangelism.

The reality is, feelings of shame and abandonment are among the most difficult for those facing exile. It may not be overt persecution that crushes your spirit or tamps down your witness; it can simply be the shame of having those closest to you consider you to be foolish, ignorant, arrogant, misguided, or a prude. Or it can be the threat of isolation, of being perpetually uninvited, unrecognized, or unwanted. Shame and the fear of exclusion combine like nothing else to quench our spirit for evangelism.

But from the perspective of 1 Peter, the antidote to a silencing shame is the hope of glory, the hope that earthly isolation and humiliation are only temporary. God, who made the world and everything in it, will one day include us in his kingdom and exalt us with the King, giving us both honor and also a home. We desperately need this future hope if we want the courage to do evangelism as exiles.

Yet all around us today Christians seem to be losing hope. We may not think we've lost it, but so often we convey an attitude of fear or frustration about changes in our society or laws. We make desperate attempts to forestall what seems to be the inevitable decline of the church in our Western society. During all of this, the world is watching our tweets and Facebook posts. They hear us grumble when we've lost the latest battle in the culture wars. They listen when our leaders lobby for what is rightfully ours, and they see us grabbing for power and recognition, for glory and honor in this life.

Confidence, assurance, and joy are the treasured possessions we often leave behind when we walk the road into exile. But I also believe the exchange can happen the other way round. Because sometimes resurrection hope is the first thing we discover when we've been freed of earthly dreams and distractions. Christians who have their hopes and worldly goods stripped from them in this life seem to have the most to teach us about a lasting hope in the next. They always seem to have the greatest joy, the deepest faith, the most invincible hope. They also seem to be most likely to proclaim that hope to others. *MISSION MINDS*

JOY IN SUFFERING

An example of this incredible joy can be found in our black sisters and brothers in Christ who suffered as slaves in America. Many times their white masters—often the very ones who introduced these Africans to the Bible—hindered them from full fellowship in the body. On Sundays, blacks might be forced to work or, if they were given rest, not permitted to worship in the white churches. Meanwhile, some slave owners also forbade them from meeting alone.

As a result, many of these believers resorted to clandestine gatherings for fellowship, preaching, and singing. They held secret church services anywhere they could get away from the watchful eye of masters, meeting in swamps, gullies, abandoned cabins, thickets, or ravines that came to be known as "hush harbors." In order to remain hidden, they would whisper as they prayed, sing behind damp quilts, or preach over a vessel of water to drown the noise.

They did this ready to suffer for Christ's name. They knew that those who were caught could expect many lashings. Masters wouldn't tolerate disobedience or insurrection. Charlotte Martin, herself a former slave, recounted how her oldest brother was once caught stealing away to a secret worship gathering. He was whipped to death.[5]

But these dangers didn't quench the Negro spirit or stifle their singing. If anything, their tortuous environment gave rise to spiritual songs of lively hope. Peter Randolph, himself a slave in the mid-1800s, chronicled in his autobiography how these underground worship services were actually an outlet for their joy in suffering and the hope of glory.

He wrote that slaves would wander off plantations to assemble in a secure location. Once everyone arrived, they would first ask each other how they were feeling. Preaching, prayer, and singing would then follow until all "generally feel quite happy." During this experience, Randolph recounted how the sufferings of the previous week would seem to temporarily vanish. As they closed the meeting, they would sing one more hymn reminding each other of the joys of heaven that awaited them and exclaim:

---

5 Mark Galli, "Defeating the Conspiracy," *Christian History* 62 (1999), 10.

"Thank God, I shall not live here always!"[6]

Throughout history and around the world, Christians who have encountered incredible suffering have exhibited incomprehensible joy. This year I had the opportunity to walk through a former prison in Romania. There, during the reign of Soviet communism, multitudes of Romanians, including many Christians, were tortured as criminals of the state. I toured cells where men were chained to the floor and forced to stand naked and upright day and night on bare, cold stone with their feet submerged in icy water.

One such political prisoner was Richard Wurmbrand, a Jewish Christian minister. He was ultimately released and later went on to found Voice of the Martyrs. But one of his memories from that time in jail is fitting here:

> It was strictly forbidden to preach to other prisoners. It was understood that whoever was caught doing this received a severe beating. A number of us decided to pay the price for the privilege of preaching, so we accepted their terms. It was a deal; we preached and they beat us. We were happy preaching. They were happy beating us, so everyone was happy.[7]

Such joy in suffering, such happiness and hope—and how that hope fueled his gospel proclamation! It's that kind of hope that's incomprehensible to Communist jailers; it's the kind of inexplicable hope that marked Negro slaves and

---

6 Peter Randolph, *From Slave Cabin to the Pulpit: The Autobiography of Rev. Peter Randolph* (Boston: James H. Earle, 1893), 202–3.

7 Richard Wurmbrand, *Tortured for Christ* (New York: Bantam, 1977), 29.

made them sing. It's a hope that can still be baffling today to doctors, counselors, classmates, or the next-door neighbor. And it's exactly the kind of hope we need to have amid our suffering and social exclusion.

But when we suffer, if our collective Christian tone is complaint, if we constantly lament our loss of cultural influence or social standing, if we weep and mourn as if Jerusalem has fallen when our chosen political agenda is overlooked, then we expose our true values. Those troubling circumstances have a way of unmasking our highest hopes. Sadly, far too often they reveal our hopes have actually been in this present age and not in the one to come.

Maybe some of you reading this book are old enough to remember when car alarms first became popular. You would be at a shopping mall and hear the scream of a blaring alarm. Everyone within earshot would suddenly stop to listen. Their heads would pop up, and they would immediately scan for the carjacker.

But nowadays car alarms are just annoying. If you're sitting in church and one goes off in the parking lot, nobody moves. Instead, we have one of two possible yet unspoken responses: *Is that my car?* or *Somebody turn that off.* We don't listen because the wailing car alarm has become a nuisance. We've learned that, more often than not, no one is stealing the car. The security system is likely overreacting to a non-issue, so we just want the noise to stop.

That's how it is with our witness. If all people hear from Christians is alarm bells, they won't listen when we actually have something important to say—when we actually have something to warn them about. They won't listen if they come to expect brash tones and useless panic.

As freedoms slip away and suffering draws near, we must not be known as an exasperated people always ready to give an answer for our protest and grievance. Our collective tone can't be like a caustic car alarm. And we must not be a people always longing for the past—for the glory days— but as those looking to a certain and truly glorious future. Then we'll have opportunities to reason with others about the hope we possess.

The reality is, in this life, the rich have reason to hope. The comfortable have every reason to hope. Beautiful people have, at least in the world's eyes, reason to hope. Powerful people have reason to hope. New England Patriots fans (this coming from a beleaguered Cleveland Browns fan) always seem to have a reason to hope. But when our hope is inexplicable, when it doesn't make sense, that's when people open their ears to hear what we have to say.

HOPE CREATES OPPORTUNITIES

That brings us to another evangelistic purpose in our hope. Peter wrote to encourage Asian believers with the hope of future glory, but he also expected that such hope would have an influence on those around them. He expected that their evident hope amid suffering would be the catalyst for many unbelievers to inquire about their faith (3:15). Because hope doesn't merely open our mouths with the gospel; visible hope can also open others' hearts to Christ.

I first met Nuri 10 years ago while riding in the back of a van through a large Asian metropolis. I quickly learned he was facing an ongoing court case because of his faith. I didn't yet speak his language, but a mutual friend introduced us and explained how Nuri had been charged with a crime against his homeland—simply for proclaiming Christ. If my friend hadn't told me the back story, I never would've guessed from Nuri's countenance that he was living as an exile in his own country. He exuded far too much joy and confidence.

Some years later—the trial now resolved—I reconnected with Nuri when I found out he had a passion for the remote Central Asian city where our family was living. Nuri had spent time there fulfilling his compulsory military service many years earlier. Ever since then, I learned, he had been praying for God to send laborers to that place, so he was eager to connect with us and support our ministry in whatever capacity he could.

For Nuri, that meant regularly traveling to our home, some 750 miles away from his own, in order to help in our outreach ministry. Whenever he came, we'd introduce him to new believers or those to whom we were witnessing. He always came with a powerful authority and positive outlook that obviously influenced those around him. In fact, when we baptized the first believers, Nuri was there in the water with us. Only years later did I learn more of Nuri's testimony, including the experience that cemented his passion for our city.

Nuri was a Muslim and had, by all accounts, a materially successful life. But at one point as a young adult he began to face emotional and mental suffering, depression, and what he describes as an utter hopelessness that made it impossible to get out of bed or go to work. After a full year of trying every possible alternative (seeing Muslim teachers, counselors, physicians, and a psychiatrist), he was ready to give up. Suicide was the only way out. But that's when Nuri cried out to God in his pain, asking for God to reveal himself.

That night, Nuri had a dream. He remembers vividly seeing an arm reached out to him to pick him up out of his trouble. But he couldn't see the man's face. Then, suddenly, he realized the man who could help him was his coworker, a man he knew was a Christian. Nuri went to him and asked if he could explain the dream. The rest, as they say, is history.

By the time Nuri entered military service and was assigned to a base in our city, he was already a passionate evangelist speaking openly to his Muslim countrymen about the hope he had found in Christ—hope that had delivered him from darkness and into light. While still a soldier, he even started a small Bible study.

One day, his commanding officer told him it had to stop. Nuri couldn't be a soldier and a Christian. In the middle of the night, the officer took him outside and beat him within inches of his life. There he lay on the ground: almost unconscious with a gun to his head. Then the officer gave him one last opportunity to deny Christ. But Nuri refused. The officer struck him again and left him helpless on the ground.

Two other soldiers who were looking on eventually came to Nuri's aid. They helped him inside. Nuri, apparently not having learned his lesson, proceeded to preach the gospel to both of them. And they believed. His hope in Christ was, and still is, contagious.

Whenever I think of Nuri's story, my mind returns to the account in Acts of Paul and Silas in Philippi (Acts 16:16–40). There, in a dark cell and chained to a wall, Paul and Silas didn't lose confidence in God. Instead, they prayed and sang hymns together, worshiping God and rejoicing in hope. Luke records that other prisoners were listening to them sing. Presumably the jailer was as well, for he was specially assigned to guard them.

An earthquake shook the prison. Doors opened. Chains broke. Paul and Silas were free. The jailer, assuming his personal prisoners had escaped, drew his sword, ready to take his own life. The shame and punishment for such a failure was likely more than he was prepared to face.

But Paul cried out to let him know they had not fled the scene. Probably shocked and in disbelief, the jailer entered the dark rubble to find Paul and Silas. He then proceeded to do what Peter said would happen when Christians exhibit a strange hope amid suffering. The jailer asked a question: "What must I do to be saved?" (Acts 16:30).

HOPE IN PRESENT PROVIDENCE

If you or I were in the same situation as Paul and Silas, I doubt we'd be singing God's praises and rejoicing in hope. More than likely our response would be to question God's purposes or doubt our understanding of God's will: "Maybe God didn't send us here after all"; "We probably shouldn't have been so bold or confrontational"; or "Did we misunderstand the Macedonian call?"

But hope for the Christian isn't just confidence in a certain, glorious future. It's hope in a present providence. It's hope that God's plans can't be thwarted by local authorities or irate mobs, by unfriendly bosses or unbelieving husbands, by Supreme Court rulings or the next election. The Christian hope is that God's purposes are so unassailable that a great thunderstorm of events can't drive them off course. Even when we're wave-tossed and lost at sea, Jesus remains the captain of the ship and the commander of the storm.

What might surprise us when we read Peter's letter is that he doesn't cast blame for his readers' exile entirely on society. He could've easily portrayed their situation and struggle as an "us vs. them" battle. Instead, Peter repeatedly suggests that God himself was behind their suffering. The rulers over them were sent by God (2:14). God is the one who gave slaves their masters, so they should, like Jesus, be mindful of God when submitting to authorities (2:19). In their suffering, they should humble themselves under God's mighty hand (5:6), because they were suffering according to God's will (4:19).

Again, this point gets back to the pattern of Jesus's own life. He entrusted himself to the Father amid suffering. Jesus, whose future was foreknown and planned by the Father, had to hope in his Father's good purposes—not just for the future joy set before him, but trusting God's perfect judgment and providence when experiencing temporary trials.

But what does hope in God's present providence have to do with evangelism?

As we've already seen, hope leads us to speak. Hope in future glory fills our hearts with joy and animates our witness, even overcoming hindrances to evangelism like shame and exclusion. But hope in God's active providence in our present circumstances also loosens our lips to preach the gospel. Why? Because we recognize that God has put us where we are "for such a time as this."[8]

Esther was a woman in literal exile. She was away from home and alone in the strange land of Persia. While her experience as a beautiful woman living in a harem was likely one of relative comfort and ease, her position was anything but desirable—especially for a God-fearing young Jewish woman. But Esther had hope. Through the influence of her cousin Mordecai, she had enough hope to risk her life for the sake of her people.

The children of Israel were in grave danger. A plot to exterminate the Jews, themselves an exiled people, was reaching full maturity under the reign of King Ahasuerus. But Esther, with her unique access to the throne, had the opportunity to influence policy. However, Esther knew that to approach his majesty on such grounds was unthinkable, even illegal. It would almost certainly be her death sentence. Yet Esther did it anyway.

Why? Because of two kinds of hope. We find them in Mordecai's encouragement to her: "For if you keep silent at this time, relief and deliverance will rise for the Jews from another place, but you and your father's house will perish. And who knows whether you have not come to the kingdom for such a time as this?" (Est. 4:14).

---

8 I find it interesting to ponder why Paul and Silas didn't run from prison immediately following the earthquake. They seem to have been thinking of the people around them, as well as God's purposes in that time and place.

Mordecai, and Esther through him, had hope in a promised future. They knew the Jewish people wouldn't be exterminated, for that would contradict God's covenant promise. So they had a future hope that couldn't be shaken. But they also had expectant confidence in God's present providence. Esther was in the king's court for a reason. Her arrival in the harem was no accident. God had brought it about—no matter how unseemly it must've been. So how was she to know whether her suffering and exile weren't planned for the salvation of God's people?

So it is with us. We may be strangers and sojourners in uncomfortable or less-than-desirable conditions. We may have had our rights and privileges stripped away from us. We may have neither the community nor the personal comfort we want. We may have been forced into unpleasant situations or relationships we'd never choose. But what if God's providential hand has put us right where we are with a specific purpose—to bring about the salvation of his own?

How can we not open our mouths and speak the gospel? How can we keep silent? If we have hope in our future and in our present, if we have a hope in God overseeing it all, then how can we not speak to our friends, neighbors, coworkers, and family members? God has put us in these places, positions, and relationships for a reason, and that reason, among others, is to proclaim the good news of Christ. Even if that means, like Esther, breaking the law and risking our necks. Even if it means conquering our greatest fear.

CHAPTER 2

FIGHTING

FEAR

WITH

FEAR

"AND IF YOU CALL ON HIM AS
FATHER WHO JUDGES IMPARTIALLY
ACCORDING TO EACH ONE'S
DEEDS, CONDUCT YOURSELVES
WITH FEAR THROUGHOUT THE
TIME OF YOUR EXILE."

—PETER THE APOSTLE (1 PET. 1:17)

It had been more than a year since we'd made the terribly difficult decision to leave our mountainous home in Central Asia. Ever since our family's tearful departure we'd been counting quarters and dreaming of the day we could make a return visit. But as it turned out, our trip came a little sooner than expected. The following autumn our good friends were getting married in two separate weddings over the same weekend in the same city at the end of a trip I'd scheduled to teach pastors in Ethiopia.

So, through the marvel of modern travel, we arranged for me to break up my itinerary—I'd cross the Red Sea to the north as my family flew eastward over the Atlantic—resulting in us arriving a few hours apart and less than a day before the first wedding.

Weeks before making the trip, I posted our travel plans on Facebook to let friends know we'd be coming their way. The goal was to see as many people as possible in a short week, though we'd prioritize opportunities to encourage the isolated believers in our former city. But when I imagined all our potential reunions, one person who didn't make my mental list was Hasan.

Hasan wasn't a Christian. He was just a friend of a friend, an acquaintance with whom I'd shared only a few passing greetings. But he was the first to respond to my post, letting me know he wanted to get together. He was willing to make it work whenever I was free. So I took his message as God's providence, and we made plans to meet.

The day came when Hasan and I settled into a discussion at a table in my favored coffee shop near his university. Our initial exchange stayed safely within the bounds of small talk, ranging from family to work, my travels to his PhD program. After 45 minutes or so, I sensed the conversation had stalled. Meanwhile, I'd been praying all day for an opportunity—one that wasn't presenting itself. Finally, at a period of silence I turned to Hasan and asked, "What exactly do you think I believe?"

Hasan knew I was a Christian (he was good friends with other believers from our house church). But I was curious what he, a Muslim, thought that meant for me. Actually, I wasn't *too* curious, because living in Central Asia had taught me that just about all Muslims had made up their minds about Christianity. They had all memorized the standard answers. But I knew I needed to nudge the conversation toward the gospel, and that initial question did the trick.

Hasan countered with the expected Islamic challenges. Our respectful debate also revealed some common misconceptions. But through it all I tried to patiently articulate the gospel, doing so clearly and with some urgency. Then, after a half hour of back and forth, Hasan paused, pulled back in his chair, and raised an exasperated question I couldn't answer: "Why didn't you ever tell me this is what you believed? Because then," he continued, "you could have had more time to explain it."

LACK OF FEAR

Most Christians would identify fear as the primary reason why we don't speak the gospel to others with more frequency or fervency. But I have my doubts. As we explored in the last chapter, I suspect the slightly more accurate reason is shame: We don't evangelize because of the expected social and emotional ramifications for us. If we're honest, the real reason we don't preach the gospel to our neighbors is because we don't want to be embarrassed. At least that was my reasoning when it came to Hasan.

From my perspective, it wouldn't make sense for me to talk with him about Christ. After all, he really wasn't a close friend. Anything I say would come across as preachy or insincere. Also, he had Christian friends. I'm sure they had talked with him about the gospel. He probably wouldn't be interested. Not to mention, if I bring up Christianity, he'll peg me as a missionary—a derogatory term for a foreigner trying to subvert his culture or undermine his country. I could lose his respect or lose the opportunity for a future relationship. Better instead to have the conversation arise organically, out of a natural relationship, all of it totally natural and anything but uncomfortable.

For many of us, when it comes to personal evangelism, comfort has usurped our calling. We speak the gospel when it seems appropriate. We open our mouths when we perceive an opportunity—that is, a willing audience. We'll bring up the topic of faith so long as it won't threaten our image, our credibility, or our relationships. If we made an honest assessment we'd have to admit we're often ashamed of our Lord. And such shame silences our witness.

That said, fear is closely related to shame and is still a real factor in our evangelism. In fact, as I'll argue in this chapter, I believe one of the greatest hindrances to evangelism is fear. Or, more accurately, *a lack of fear*. As feelings of anxiety and dread well up within us and drown out our evangelistic zeal, the solution isn't to eliminate all fears. Our absence of appropriate fear is actually part of the problem. The solution we find in 1 Peter is to fight fear with fear—to grow in our fear of God and our fear *for* (not *of*) our fellow man.

Now, you might question such thinking. After all, doesn't the Bible say perfect love casts out fear? Is there really any place for fear in the Christian life? Doesn't God's unconditional love (a concept we will return to in chapter 5) mean we have nothing to fear but fear itself?

But here's where we encounter some of the strangeness of Peter's first epistle. Because as he wrote to exiled Christians encompassed by fears small and great, Peter repeatedly encouraged them *to fear*. Such an approach, at least to our American mindset, seems counter-intuitive if not counter-productive. If we were writing a letter to instill hope in struggling Christians, we wouldn't think to encourage them *to fear*.

It's not as though Peter didn't recognize the negative repercussions of fear for those experiencing social exclusion. He didn't want his readers to be afraid (3:6). Even amid real suffering, he exhorted them not to fear or be troubled by their opponents (3:14). But Peter also challenged them to conduct their lives *with fear* throughout their exile (1:17). Rather than releasing any and all sense of fear, he expected them to chart their course through shadowy exile by the constant lodestar of Godward fear.

We should also note that for Peter such God-directed fear was in no way contradictory to hope.[9] In what is likely the most well-known passage on evangelism and apologetics from 1 Peter, we often miss the strong link between hope and fear. In the preceding verse, Peter began by writing that Christians shouldn't fear opposition. Rather, "in your hearts honor Christ the Lord as holy, always being prepared to make a defense to anyone who asks you for a reason for the hope that is in you; yet do it with gentleness and respect" (3:15).[10] In other words, being ready with the gospel is directly connected to these two dispositions: (1) not fearing others, and instead (2) honoring Christ as holy.

We need to take a moment and examine this second idea. We get number one. Don't be afraid. That makes sense for our evangelistic efforts. But what does it mean to honor the Lord as holy? What is Peter referring to when he uses this curious phrase?

---

[9] Peter connects fear and hope in 3:5–6, 3:14–15, and 1:17–21.

[10] The word translated "respect" in 3:15 is *phobos*, the same Greek word which occurs in 3:14 referring to the "fear" they shouldn't have toward their opponents.

First of all, the verb he uses hearkens back to the Lord's Prayer where Jesus teaches us to ask for God's name to be hallowed—to be honored as holy. But that doesn't take us back far enough. Writing centuries earlier, Isaiah prophesied of the coming Assyrian invasion by which Israel would be taken captive and exiled. Then God gave Isaiah this personal word of instruction: "Do not fear what they fear, nor be in dread. But the LORD of hosts, him you shall honor as holy. Let him be your fear, and let him be your dread" (Isa. 8:12–13).[11]

Isaiah had been commissioned by God to preach a message that would mostly fall on deaf ears. It was a message predicting God's judgment and the people's ruin, as well as the hope of future salvation. But given that commission, Isaiah wasn't to succumb to his hearers' fears: the fear of their opponents or the fear of rejection. Instead, Isaiah was to honor the Lord as holy. To put it another way, he was to let God be his greatest dread, the fear above all fears.[12]

Bringing that idea forward into the letter of 1 Peter, we see the apostle's implicit reasoning by his use of Isaiah's verbiage. We see that being ready with the gospel doesn't involve completely eliminating our dread, but redirecting it. We recognize the greatest hindrance to our evangelism isn't necessarily a stifling fear, but a lack of fear. This revelation helps us understand how fearing God can actually be the remedy to any and all fears which would otherwise silence our witness.

---

11 This same passage speaks of a stone of stumbling and rock of offense, earlier referenced by Peter in 2:8.

12 Jeremiah's calling mirrored that of Isaiah in that he was sent to preach to those who would oppose his message, but God challenged him by saying, "Do not be dismayed by them, lest I dismay you before them" (Jer. 1:17).

PREACHING SCARED

Yusuf was our family's pastor for about a year. An endearing older gentlemen, he possesses the kind of grandfatherly disposition that can warm any child's heart, the sort of glad-hearted greeting that can make any stranger an instant friend. Hidden within his small stature he also conceals a booming voice fit for the largest audiences in the grandest halls. However, Yusuf only has a small flock, a congregation of about 30 that gathers in a nondescript basement apartment in the midst of a sprawling Central Asian metropolis. His little church was less than a one-mile walk from our first home overseas.

On my introduction to Pastor Yusuf, he welcomed me into his church and showed me a Bible on his desk, complete with an unmistakable bullet hole—a real conversation starter for what he'd endured as a minister of the gospel. Not too long after that first meeting, our family joined his fellowship in what became one of the fondest years of our ministry.

During our time there, on a Saturday evening before Easter, Yusuf sat in his small church office preparing and praying for the coming Lord's Day. That's when he heard a commotion outside and a call at the gate. He rose from his study, opened the screeching metal door, and climbed the concrete steps into the night air. There at the front entrance was a group of young men waiting for him.

What happened next was a mixture of the shocking and predictable. The young thugs immediately launched into a tirade of hate-filled speech, threatening Pastor Yusuf. They said his church had no place in their Muslim community.

They accosted him for corrupting the neighborhood. They told him he and his church were no longer welcome. Then, almost without warning, one ruffian kicked him in the chest, knocking Yusuf's small frame backwards. He tumbled down the concrete stair. The assailants fled.

The next morning when we arrived for church ready to celebrate our Lord's resurrection, we were met with news of the attack. Members spoke in hushed tones, wondering who had done this and if it was an isolated event. We were concerned about our pastor's condition, as well as the danger for our own gathering on a day of such significance to potential attackers. The joy of Easter was quickly threatened by genuine fear.

But by the time our worship began, nerves seemed to have settled a bit. We all took our places, including Pastor Yusuf sitting in his usual front-row seat. The service opened with prayer and song. Then, about halfway through the time of worship, a group of three men entered the back door. We had visitors.

In much of the world today, having visitors at church means something totally different from what it does in our comfortable American context. The whole situation can be a bit tricky. Are they friendly? Are they government officials or informants? Could they be seekers? Or terrorists? So whoever it is, you greet them with a smile—and fervent prayer.

But this particular day we were especially on edge. I remember how, as the three men sat directly behind my wife and three young kids, a million scenarios raced through my mind. My throat tightened while I voiced the words of the hymn. When other members slowly turned to notice the guests, tension clouded the room. But I could also tell that Yusuf still didn't know they were there.

As the final song came to a close, our pastor stood and approached the front. He opened his Bible, turned, and looked up. Then he saw them. We all noticed him notice them. No one knew what would happen next. What, if anything, would the strangers do? How would Yusuf respond? What were we to do?

After an initial pause that seemed like ages, Pastor Yusuf launched into his sermon. To this day I don't actually know what he had prepared to preach that Easter Sunday, but I suspect his topic shifted. With trembling in his voice he immediately spoke of Christ and the gospel, his death and resurrection, and the need for all people to repent and believe. His tone was forceful. His eyes locked to the congregation. I sensed his gaze focus past my brow and directly to our visitors. Yusuf had taken inventory of the fear in the room and he decided to stock the shelves with an even greater fear: the coming judgment of God. His Spirit-filled boldness was amazing.

COMING JUDGMENT

Jesus knew that in such terrifying moments we'd be tempted to swallow our tongues. But he warned that all who are ashamed of him before others would have the Son of Man ashamed of them when he comes in glory (Luke 9:26). Jesus called us to shake off ours fears when maligned and threatened by the world. We must neither be afraid of our hearers nor embarrassed by Christ. Why? Because only then will we have the chutzpah to speak a message that's regarded as foolishness to the wise and weakness to the strong (1 Cor. 1:18–31).

But Jesus had more to say. According to Matthew, as he sent out his chosen disciples with a message to proclaim, he called them to fear something greater than their worst enemies—they were to fear God and his coming judgment:

> So have no fear of them, for nothing is covered that will not be revealed, or hidden that will not be known. What I tell you in the dark, say in the light, and what you hear whispered, proclaim on the housetops. And do not fear those who kill the body but cannot kill the soul. Rather fear him who can destroy both soul and body in hell. (Matt. 10:26–28)

If you read through a collection of old Negro spirituals, you'll observe that those beleaguered slaves sang about judgment and damnation in ways that would cause most of us to blush. Their ability to harness the passions of the imprecatory psalms and simultaneously drive them toward an evangelistic appeal is astonishing, if not jarring. In one line they can revel in God's retribution; in the next they can summon sinners to repent.

How could they do this? I suspect it's much like their hope-filled hymnody. Just as those who face earthly shame grow in their expectation of eternal glory, those who suffer under constant fears and injustice have a greater anticipation for the coming Judge of all the earth. Those well acquainted with earthly terrors—if you have a chance to meet them—have a keener sense of the fear of God, a greater wakefulness to his wrath. Their earthly troubles and sorrows can easily lead them to long for the day of reckoning.

So it'll likely be for us. As fears increase in the American church, we'll have the opportunity to resurrect a holy fear of God in our midst. As we suffer under the temporal judgment of God as weary sojourners, we may just find a stronger voice to warn others to flee from the wrath to come. As we sense the nearness of the day of retribution, we may speak once again with unction and holy disquiet.

But over the last decades, in our efforts at evangelism and church growth in the West, the characteristic most glaringly absent has been this: the fear of God. We've believed the most effective witness for Christ is positive and encouraging. We've assumed the way to win the masses is by rebranding our churches and offering people a better life. We've believed our greatest apologists are successful CEOs or professional athletes. The gospel has become one-dimensional: it's all about accessing blessing without the need to avoid judgment.

Yet in the book of Acts, the early church grew and flourished as they lived in the fear of the Lord (Acts 9:31). The apostle Paul wrote to the Corinthian believers, calling them to be ambassadors for Christ in view of God's judgment. "Knowing the fear of the Lord," he explained, "we persuade others" (2 Cor. 5:11). Jude also encouraged us to save others by clutching them from the fire, showing mercy *with fear* (Jude 23).

This was also the perspective of Peter writing to exiled Christians in ancient Asia. They were experiencing shame and reproach. Like their Savior, they were rejected by the world and maligned for good deeds. Their suffering and trials, at one level, could even be described by Peter as God's judgment. Through ongoing difficulties and flaming opposition, the Father was actively working to refine and purify them. But if such judgment comes on God's people, "what will be the outcome for those who do not obey the gospel of God?" (4:17). This is why the gospel must be proclaimed, because all will give an account to One who is ready to judge the living and the dead (4:5–6).

Have we really taken into account the end and outcome for our friends, relatives, neighbors, and coworkers? Is our failure to evangelize really an issue of fearing too much, or not fearing nearly enough? Do we cherish our comfort and others' respect more than we cherish God's glory and their deliverance? Will we love them enough to fear *for them*, to show them mercy and kindness by warning them and snatching them out of the fire? The consistent testimony of the New Testament is that if we have the appropriate fear for them *and of God*, we'll preach the gospel. We'll speak out and not be ashamed.

WE PLEASE THOSE WE FEAR

But what does it actually look like to fear God? Am I suggesting that the Christian life demands we walk around with a Bible in one hand and a lightning rod in the other? Conversely, am I suggesting that bold evangelism involves shouting down strangers on a street corner with warnings of impending doom, or venting on social media about the wickedness of sin?

To get an answer, I think we can actually learn something from our experience. When we observe that our problem in evangelism is fearing others too much, we should note the form such fear takes. We typically aren't running from people in terror. We aren't cowering in a corner.[13] More often than not, we're not even faced with the kind of fear Yusuf experienced. Rather, fearing others more than God usually demonstrates itself in trying to please them more than God. To put it another way, you know you fear someone when you desire their approval and live for their praise.

But as we explored last chapter, the Christian in exile is called to embrace the shame and social humiliation that comes as a package deal with the cross. We're called to live for the approval and honor of King Jesus alone. We're to be first and foremost God-pleasers and not—as the old King James Version says—man-pleasers (Gal. 1:10). In fact, Paul's letter to the Colossians is helpful to see this connection. He wrote that servants shouldn't live to please their masters but fear God (Col. 3:22). In other words, fearing is paralleled with pleasing. We seek to please most those we fear most.

Here again, Scripture connects this heart attitude and disposition with faithful gospel proclamation. Christians who try to please people ultimately fail at pleasing God and fail at proclaiming his gospel.[14] And far too often this is the problem in our evangelistic endeavors: We're fundamentally committed to keeping people happy and having them like us, having them think we're smart, contemporary, hip, tolerant,

---

13 In the same way, fearing God in the Bible doesn't mean avoiding him. It's evidenced by our desire to please, live for, and be with him.

14 See 1 Thess. 2:4 and Gal. 1:10.

progressive, fun, approving—and the list goes on. We want to please them, and we want them to approve of us. As was the case for me with Hasan, we can fear losing a friendship more than we fear losing a friend.

We withhold the truth for the sake of acceptance. We polish our social media persona to remove the rough edges of religiosity. And we nurture relationships with unbelievers for years without broaching the subject of Christ. Why? To please people. In our twisted understanding, we reason such people-pleasing efforts are for the sake of future gospel opportunities. But in reality, we're often just fearing others instead of God.[15]

FEARING GOD AMID AND ABOVE ALL FEARS

In calling his readers to fear God and not others, Peter was in no way naïve about the cost involved. He wasn't glossing over real trials. He wasn't ignorant about what it means to lose friends over the gospel.[16] After all, as we've come to see, he labeled such relational discord and emotional injury as harsh *exile*.

In the same way, I don't intend to downplay the challenge this call to preach the gospel brings for us. Nor would I wish to insinuate that the soft persecution we face is insignificant.

---

15 Some helpful resources on this topic would include Lou Priolo, *Pleasing People: How Not to Be an Approval Junkie* (Phillipsburg, NJ: P&R, 2007); Ed Welch, *When People Are Big and God is Small: Overcoming Peer Pressure, Codependency, and the Fear of Man* (Phillipsburg, NJ: P&R, 1997).

16 Paul challenged Peter for his people-pleasing that initially led Peter to misrepresent the good news.

I'm also not suggesting that we in America don't have substantial cause for alarm in our own land. In fact, it's one primary reason for writing this book—our entrance into fearful exile *is happening now*.

Yes, Christians in America are increasingly isolated and denigrated. Yes, our cultural and social capital is vanishing before our eyes. Yes, in the span of one short week the Supreme Court could easily rewrite our futures and remove many freedoms. Yes, public school curricula are being weaponized to indoctrinate children in secular dogma and a new sexual ethic. It doesn't even take much imagination to envision how well-intentioned laws against discrimination, hate speech, or terrorism could one day be used to justify the imprisonment of Christians. And it doesn't end there.

On a personal level, we have plenty more room for fear. By standing up for Christ we run the risk of forfeiting promotions or positions, of missing out on tenure or a contract. We might even lose our families. But this shouldn't surprise us. Jesus said he didn't come to bring peace but a sword (Matt. 10:34). We have much to lose.

Yet none of that—none of that—justifies Christians being terrified. We must not, according to Peter, tremble in fear at the thought of surrendering a job or business, at a failed school board initiative or a particular Supreme Court decision. Because if we do, we're preaching the completely wrong gospel to the world. We're telling them our greatest fear is the loss of money and power and influence, the loss of our beloved comfort. But as long as that is the case, we show that our fear (and our gospel) is no different from theirs.

Nehemiah was a man surrounded by danger. The biblical book that bears his name begins with him in exile under Persian rule. The remainder of the story focuses on Nehemiah's time in Israel as he sought to rebuild the walls of Jerusalem. However, back at home, Nehemiah was still a stranger and sojourner, though now in his own land. His attempts to lead the people to restore the holy city were constantly under threat. His opponents were unrelenting in their criticism and activism against his efforts. In fact, we read that their explicit goal was to frighten him (Neh. 6:19).

But the book of Nehemiah is also the record of a man who feared God more than people. His courageous and benevolent leadership, his commitment to God's glory, and his ultimate success were owing to his all-surpassing reverence for God. It was the kind of fearful faith that led his followers as they were surrounded by blood-thirsty enemies, saying: "Do not be afraid of them. Remember the Lord, who is great and awesome" (Neh. 4:14).[17] Through his fiery trials and amid earthly fears, Nehemiah's perspective was the same as Isaiah's before him: Don't be afraid; fear God.

This became the motif of Peter's letter written to a community of exiles—not removed from their land, but living normal, everyday lives in their hometowns while surrounded by countless opponents. Their exile was one of constant criticism and reviling. They were mocked for foolhardy faith

---

[17] This verse seems to hearken back to Moses's similar instruction to Israel in relation to the surrounding nations of Canaan from Deut. 7:21. It's not immediately clear from the English translation of Neh. 4:14, but the word that refers to God and is translated as "awesome" is the Hebrew *yare'*, the same word also translated "afraid" in this verse. So Nehemiah was calling his fellow citizens to remember their dreadful and awesome God rather than fear their opponents. In fact, the whole book of Nehemiah is a story about overcoming the fear of man with the fear of God.

and slurred for clean living. Their opponents slandered them and, perhaps like Nehemiah's adversaries, would've liked nothing more than to have them shaking in their boots.

But Peter called his readers not to dread anything that might frighten them (3:6). What's especially interesting is how he did this with a level of nuance. Peter called for slaves to respect[18] their masters, but to do so "mindful of God." He instructed wives to be subject to their unbelieving husbands with the same respect, yet not exhibit fear in doing so. He also recognized the need to honor human authorities, even the godless Roman emperor. But Christians were not to honor him in the same way they feared God (2:17).

In a world teeming with reasons to be terrified, the only rightful recipient of our fear, according to Peter, is God. So as we consider our heart-disposition in speaking with neighbors and friends about Christ, we must keep this distinction in our minds: We fear God, not people. We aim to please him, not others. We seek his approval; he alone deserves our highest respect.

That fear of him, along with a fear of coming judgment, is a compelling motivation to open our mouths with the gospel. But we do not open our mouths with hate-filled bigotry, with arrogant condescension, or with brimstone on our breath. According to Peter, we fear God *and* honor everyone else. So as we take the gospel to others, even to our opponents, we're called to approach them with kindness, gentleness, and respect.

---

18 The word translated "respect" in relation to masters, husbands, and others is from the Greek *phobos*, which can also be translated "fear." So there is a measure of fear (respect) that is appropriate for human institutions and authorities but which is categorically different from the fear that God demands.

WITH

RESPECT

FOR ALL

"BE SUBJECT FOR THE LORD'S SAKE TO EVERY HUMAN INSTITUTION, WHETHER IT BE TO THE EMPEROR AS SUPREME, OR TO GOVERNORS AS SENT BY HIM TO PUNISH THOSE WHO DO EVIL AND TO PRAISE THOSE WHO DO GOOD. FOR THIS IS THE WILL OF GOD, THAT BY DOING GOOD YOU SHOULD PUT TO SILENCE THE IGNORANCE OF FOOLISH PEOPLE. LIVE AS PEOPLE WHO ARE FREE, NOT USING YOUR FREEDOM AS A COVER-UP FOR EVIL, BUT LIVING AS SERVANTS OF GOD. HONOR EVERYONE. LOVE THE BROTHERHOOD. FEAR GOD. HONOR THE EMPEROR."

—PETER THE APOSTLE (1 PET. 2:13-17)

Two hours away from our former home, a barren stretch of highway ribbons westward through ravines and craggy massifs until it gradually opens to a broad plain and to civilization—a city of about 100,000 that, as of five years ago, was home to exactly one follower of Christ.

Aisha lived there without any church, much less a single Christian friend. We first learned about her situation through an acquaintance who knew her 10 years earlier, back when Aisha was a new convert. But they had since lost regular contact, so we set out to find this sister in the Lord separated from us by some 120 miles.

After eventually reaching Aisha via phone, we traveled to visit her. Under a leafy canopy in the middle of a city park, we sat at a picnic table sharing tea and stories. It was then, at our first meeting, that I realized just how lonely she was. Her unbelieving husband, Metin, was in prison. Meanwhile, her two grown children were away at college. She was entirely alone.

As much as possible, I tried to encourage Aisha while trying to grasp what life as a disciple of Christ looks like when you have no possibility for believing community. If anyone was ever a Christian exile, she was. And the result, as you might imagine, was threadbare faith for Aisha.

Over the next several months we did what we could to stay connected. We invited her to our city, and she would take the nauseating bus ride through mountain passes to see us. Or, more often the case, we would drive to see her. But one particular day I remember receiving a WhatsApp message from Aisha. Her husband had been released from jail, and she wanted us to meet him. So Aisha suggested we bring the whole family, kids and all, and stay with her over the weekend.

As parents, we didn't know what to do. What are the appropriate risks to your family when trying to bring the gospel to a city—or just one person? At this point we hardly knew Aisha, and Metin was a convicted criminal. Do you take your young girls to sleep in the home of a felon? We also suspected that Aisha didn't have beds for all of us. This clearly wasn't going to be a relaxing getaway. But we accepted.

That first evening our introduction to Metin went smoothly. He was anything but shy, his chattiness perhaps owing to extended time in prison. We talked at length about everything: the weather, his work, politics, religion, even art. He showed us multiple oil paintings he'd completed during his incarceration. The portraits showed some real skill, though they were more valuable as a window into his past.

The next morning Aisha made us all breakfast. Later we walked around town. Then we picnicked at the park. Metin grilled up our kids' favorite: succulent lamb and spicy chicken wings, plus eggplant, peppers, and tomatoes. We spent hours together but never really broached his run-in with the law. We just did our best to treat him as a person, someone we were happy to meet as the husband of our dear sister in Christ. And, of course, we were praying all along—for our safety and his salvation.

WINNING OTHERS
WITHOUT WORDS

When Peter composed his letter to suffering believers in first century Asia, he had in mind women exactly like Aisha. His concern was their position of weakness and isolation, and he encouraged them to relate to their unbelieving husbands with humility and gentleness. The goal was their spouse's salvation.[19] As such, his full instruction to these women provides a perfect case study for how we can conduct evangelism as exiles:

---

19 We should note that Peter's encouragements to gentleness and humility were for the purpose of promoting their witness and thus don't represent a comprehensive Christian approach to situations of domestic violence or sexual abuse. We also shouldn't overlook the subtly subversive and culturally surprising disposition Peter calls for by encouraging these women to not follow their husbands in religious matters but seek instead their conversion to Christ.

> Likewise, wives, be subject to your own husbands, so
> that even if some do not obey the word, they may be
> won without a word by the conduct of their wives, when
> they see your respectful and pure conduct. Do not let
> your adorning be external—the braiding of hair and the
> putting on of gold jewelry, or the clothing you wear—but
> let your adorning be the hidden person of the heart with
> the imperishable beauty of a gentle and quiet spirit,
> which in God's sight is very precious. For this is how the
> holy women who hoped in God used to adorn themselves,
> by submitting to their own husbands, as Sarah obeyed
> Abraham, calling him lord. And you are her children, if
> you do good and do not fear anything that is frightening.
> (3:1–6)

In this short passage we see several themes found
throughout the entire letter. Peter spoke of *holy* women who
hope in God, who *don't fear* anything, and who *respectfully
submit* to their husbands for the sake of the gospel. Such
godly and courageous women show the posture of an exiled
evangelist.

What took priority, though, in Peter's address to these wives
was respect for their husbands. This particular section
continues Peter's extended discussion on submitting
to authority. As such, we should see that their humble
decorum—their "gentle and quiet spirit"—was meant
to adorn the gospel before their husbands. And Peter
understood that their respectful disposition was of such
importance—it was so effectual—that their husbands
could be brought to faith in Christ by merely watching the
consistent respect of their wives. When they demonstrated
a surprisingly humble submission, these hope-filled wives

could win their husbands *without a word*.[20]

I've spent extended time with many believers like Aisha who suffer in the loneliness and isolation of a single-believer household. Especially in the case of first-generation Christians, it can be incredibly difficult to live in the same four walls as others who oppose the gospel. Not only do they not believe like you do, they can also use their collective influence to manipulate, shame, exclude, provoke, and intimidate.

But Peter called those in such a difficult situation to live with the utmost respect, dignity, patience, gentleness, quietness, and humility. And while we might think Peter was asking a lot of these women, the reality is he expected the exact same disposition of all believers—even us—as we live as strangers and sojourners in this world.

HONOR FOR EVERYONE

As mentioned above, Peter's specific instruction to believing wives is part of a larger section on the Christian posture toward all people. Humility and gentleness aren't just the appropriate approach of a woman in a patriarchal society. It's also not just the necessary attitude of slaves living under lopsided authority. No, all Christians everywhere are called to *honor everyone*.

This can be incredibly difficult when we feel pushed into

---

20 Being won "without a word" doesn't imply these husbands could believe a gospel they never heard. According to Peter, these men already knew the Word but had not obeyed it. Therefore, we can't use this passage to justify the worn-out and wrongheaded advice on evangelism to "preach the gospel and if necessary use words."

orner as exiles. When criticized and scorned, we often respond in kind. That's because the natural inclination of every human heart is to play dodgeball with shame. If we're mocked, then we'll mock back. If we're trolled, then we'll be sure to troll back—only one better. But Jesus left us a different example. When he was reviled, he didn't revile in return (2:22–23).

Furthermore, Peter didn't simply challenge his suffering readers to passively receive the world's abuse, as if that's what it means to turn the other cheek. Instead, we're to actively pursue honor.[21] We're to seek peace (3:11). We're to bless and not curse (3:9). We're to respect our authorities and dignify our enemies, whether they be deadbeat dads or despots. So yes, according to Peter, we're to *honor everyone*.

Take a moment and turn that thought over in your mind. You're called to show honor to every single person. Not just the people who deserve it. Not just those who earn our respect. Not just the ones who treat us agreeably. Not just the politicians we vote for or the immigrants who are legal. Not just the customers who pay their bills or the employees who do their work. Not just the neighborly neighbors. Not just kind pagans or honest Muslims. Not just the helpful wife or the good father.

As Peter wrote to servants who suffered unjustly, what good is it if we're only nice to the people who are nice to us? Rather, it's a true sign of God's grace in our lives when we can be respectfully submissive to unpleasant and unfair

---

21 As Jesus said, if someone would seek your tunic, let him have your cloak as well (Matt. 5:40).

authority (2:18–20), when we do to others as we wish they did to us (Matt. 7:12).

It's also important to note that Peter didn't merely write to people languishing under oppressive leadership—whether governmental, occupational, or domestic—as if the only people called to a humble disposition are those of low estate. No, he wrote to all kinds of Christian exiles, people who were mocked by their peers. He wrote to believers who were slandered by their neighbors and friends.

Perhaps after reading the last chapter some concluded that since we don't fear others, and since we don't try to please them, we don't care what they think or feel.[22] That when we preach the gospel, we shame others. That the Bible gives us permission to bludgeon unbelievers with our doctrine and their sin. Or that we have a pass to criticize our enemies and their causes, dragging them behind us in the dust of our righteous ridicule.

I doubt many of us are guilty of browbeating anyone with the gospel. But if we're honest, we're often culpable for not respecting our opponents. For not showing due honor. For using our words to shame our enemies or attack their agendas. For casually slandering those with whom we disagree, even rejoicing when our sarcasm gets laughs or our meme gets likes.

It should be noteworthy to us, then, that from the outset of

---

22 Paul, who spoke ardently about not pleasing others, also modeled an appropriate kind of people-pleasing for the sake of their salvation (1 Cor. 10:33). So there must be an appropriate social or cultural accommodation that makes the gospel more clear, while other forms of accommodation ultimately undermine our evangelistic endeavors.

his letter Peter was concerned that his readers who faced regular insult for their faith be quick to "put away all malice and all deceit and hypocrisy and envy and all slander" (2:1). Those are strong and comprehensive words. But Peter knew that Christian exiles easily slip into an unending volley of tit for tat. Of hurting those who hurt them. Of showing spite to their accusers. Of harboring malice toward those who put them down. Of mentally standing on their toes, like a tennis player, ready to return serve.

WITH GENTLENESS AND RESPECT

But Peter wrote his letter so we'd have a different kind of readiness. He wants us to be prepared to give an answer for the hope in us—yet do so with gentleness and respect (3:15). As we have already explored, such gospel preparedness comes from fearing God first and demonstrating an evident hope. But our manner of speech should also exhibit a certain kind of fear toward those to whom we witness, a gentle spirit and a humble respect. Such a disposition is critical for exiled evangelists.

Just as our enduring hope can be a compelling testimony when we suffer, showing respect to our rivals has a way of validating the gospel we preach. Many times people won't be compelled to listen to our message on account of sound arguments or persuasive evidence. Instead, their ears will only open when we demonstrate inexplicable kindness, meekness, and compassion.

The fact is, ridiculing your opponents is the privilege of the powerful. But now, as an excluded minority, American

Christians no longer have the upper hand. Maligning our cultural and religious adversaries is therefore no longer an effective strategy. The days of mocking atheists, crass joking about homosexuals, slurring Muslims, and making derogatory remarks about political rivals need to end. They should have never existed. But the church could get away with such impudence when we were the cultural majority. Not anymore.

As we face increasing opposition, we can either turn up the volume on our vitriol, or we can follow the instruction of Peter and put aside all malice and slander. We can approach our enemies with gentleness and respect. And if we do, we'll have an incredible opportunity for the gospel.

James Lankford, a believing U.S. Senator from Oklahoma, recently spoke to this issue in an interview with *Christianity Today*.[23] He specifically referenced the stunning words of 1 Peter, linking the testimony of our lives with honoring authority—even the godless authority of a Roman emperor. As he suggested, if Peter could call his readers to honor Caesar, do we really think we can get away with dishonoring our own authorities?

Lankford then went on to critique the pervasive culture of disrespect in Washington. But he suggested that this culture presents Christians with a unique opportunity to be truly revolutionary. Because, as he has experienced first-hand, if you show honor to others it provides an opportunity for the gospel.

---

23 "On Being an Evangelical Senator During the Trump Presidency," *Christianity Today*, March 21, 2018. https://www.christianitytoday.com/ct/2018/march-web-only/james-lankford-senator-oklahoma-evangelical-trump.html

But we must admit that glad-hearted respect isn't our normal response. The American cultural proclivity to reject authority and put down opponents has bled into the church, staining all our attempts to win a hearing for the gospel. So if we truly desire an open door for evangelism, we in the church can't be those who sling mud on political rivals and throw shade on their followers. We can't succumb to the rancor of the 24/7 news cycle. Perhaps most important of all, we can't dishonor our opponents by dehumanizing them.

In my observation, our social dialogue naturally slides toward such dehumanization, especially in a technological age that's disconnected from personal relationship and the natural decorum that often flows from it.[24] Social media are the prime example of disconnection, functioning like the digital version of bumper-sticker Christianity. On these media we parade our views on any number of issues with casual indignity. After all, we won't ever see half the people who read our tweets. But we also won't know half the disrepute we bring to Jesus's name. It's just like a shiny, chrome fish symbol stuck on a lift gate that has been crowded out by tacky, passive-aggressive decals. Our gospel is obscured.

SILENT FOR THE SAKE OF THE GOSPEL

For this reason, I think one of the most important lessons we can learn is the virtue of silence. This lesson became most clear to me in Central Asia as I met regularly with a few engineering professors at our local university. These men

---

24 For a more detailed reflection on this reality, see Alan Jacobs, *How to Think: A Survival Guide for a World at Odds* (New York: Currency, 2017).

were highly intelligent, deeply spiritual, and committed to their Islamic faith. However, they were also open to religious dialogue such that they were willing to meet once a week to discuss Christianity.

On Wednesday nights we'd gather around a cluttered desk in one instructor's small office, sipping tea and debating religion for hours on end. After a few weeks of back and forth, we eventually settled on a format where we'd discuss a chosen topic (such as obedience, judgment, sacrifice, or end times). Both sides would come prepared to describe how their holy book addressed the given subject.

The format worked well (particularly as a means to highlight the unique Christian gospel). We were able to dialogue respectfully, taking time to humbly learn each other's core beliefs (sometimes finding points of agreement), but also having the opportunity to argue for our own perspective. However, some nights the discussion inevitably strayed from our appointed topic. Current events or politics would take over.

One particular subject that repeatedly crept in was the 9/11 attacks in New York. These professors were convinced that George Bush, aided by Jews infiltrating the American government, had planned and executed the destruction of the Twin Towers. It was all a cunning ruse to demonize Muslims at home and advance a Western imperialist agenda abroad. And they had YouTube videos to prove it.

It's amazing what emotions can well up within an American citizen when a group of Muslim men insists that your government has plotted against its own people and committed mass murder in order to wage a greater war on Islam. The very idea made me ill. I wanted to lash out with the best arguments I could muster, or at least come back the next week prepped and ready to demolish their theory. But I didn't. I couldn't.

I couldn't allow my national pride or a commitment to "the facts" to jeopardize my greater commitment—to humbly present the gospel.

When we seek to do evangelism as exiles, we already have a really hard sell. We're trying to convince people that a Jewish carpenter was God's Son, come from heaven to die for our sins. He was buried, and three days later he rose from the dead and now reigns over all. Not only that, we're also calling them to join us as social outcasts. Must we also try to persuade them about matters of history or geopolitics? Do we really want to argue for our opinion on the environment or economics? Or could those hobby-horse topics end up as barriers to Christ's gospel?

Please don't hear me say that Christians should never address controversial topics. Or that we shouldn't speak out against evil and injustice. Of course we should. But the value of silence still stands. It's a lesson I'm even trying to learn as a parent: You have to pick your battles. You can't take offense at every turn. You can't address every problem or every infraction. And most of all, the dominant message must not be constant displeasure or disagreement. Otherwise we'll lose our audience before we get to the most important message of all.

We must learn to triage our agendas. We must learn to

prioritize our preaching. Some things are of higher value; others are likely not even worthy of comment. Because as much as people can be won to Christ through our witness, they can also be lost by our words. Our endless social commentary and political engagement can be off-putting. So better to be quiet and respectful than bold and boorish. Better to sometimes be silent.

You probably wouldn't expect a book on evangelism to talk about the necessity of being quiet for the sake of the gospel. But this is exactly what Peter advocates for in his instruction to believing wives. And I think it applies to more than just their situations.

The apostle Paul, addressing Timothy and the Ephesian church, wrote that prayers should be made for all people, specifically those in authority. The purpose of those prayers was that Christians might lead a peaceable and quiet life, godly and dignified in every way. But even that doesn't seem to be Paul's ultimate purpose. He concluded that this approach is good because God desires all people to be saved (1 Tim. 2:1–6). In other words, the ultimate goal of prayerful respect and a quiet life is seeing all kinds of people saved.[25]

In a similar vein, Paul wrote to his protégé Timothy to avoid needless controversies and endless debates—again for the sake of the gospel. The servant of the Lord, he insisted, shouldn't be quarrelsome, but *kind to everyone*, patiently enduring evil. What was the reason for such a passive

---

[25] This passage shouldn't be understood to suggest that our responsibility to live in godliness depends upon external circumstances and peace. Christians are nowhere told that their behavior and witness are ultimately governed by their situation. As Knight observes, the "quiet" prayed for is for the sake of the gospel, though it "does not mean a sheltered life." Knight, *The Pastoral Epistles* (Grand Rapids: Eerdmans, 1992), 117.

approach from Paul, the flaming evangelist? "God may perhaps grant them repentance leading to a knowledge of the truth" (2 Tim. 2:23–25).

So, again, we should highlight that gentleness and respect aren't just the requisite deportment of women and slaves who wish to magnify Christ. This is for all of us. We must be kind to all. We must honor all. We must shun the invitation to speak out on every issue, defend every position, or answer every opponent, because God may use such silence to save others.

BLESS AND DO NOT CURSE

We still haven't really talked about what it actually means to respect others. For me, describing disrespect is easier than defining honor. That's likely owing to the fact that honor as a virtue is lacking in Western culture. We don't have a plethora of good examples. But Paul's instruction to the church in Rome (which mirrors Peter's in many ways) can help us fill out some of what it means to honor our opponents. Below is my own paraphrase of his words to believers living in that hostile environment:[26]

> Bless those who persecute you. Be kind to them with your words and wish them well. Don't curse them to their face or berate them behind their back. Instead, when

---

26 Rom. 12:14–21 represents a distinct unit of instruction regarding believers' relationship with non-believers. According to Dunn, "In vv 14–21 Paul broadens his perspective from the internal relationships within and among the Christian congregations to take in their relationships with the wider community within which they had to live" as an "endangered species." He also notes how Paul, certainly aware of hostility and provocations against the believers, does not merely call for "passive resistance" but "a positive outgoing goodness in response." Dunn, *Romans 9–16*, Word Biblical Commentary 38B (Dallas: Word, 1988), 755.

they are happy, be happy for them, even *with them*.[27] Rejoice at their successes, and tell them how glad you are when they get a raise or a new grandbaby. Be sorry for their losses. Weep and mourn when they are sorrowful, when they lose a loved one or even suffer the natural consequences of their sin. Don't say, "Serves you right." Instead, live in harmony with one another. Do what you can to get along. Don't look for ways to spite them, and don't create unnecessary strife. That would be a proud attitude. You are no better than them, so be humble toward everyone. Associate with people beneath you. Dignify the poor and the ill. Show lavish honor to your employees and contractors and vendors, to your babysitter and to children. Take time to talk with the people no one else will. Don't be too big for your own britches, and don't take other people's bad behavior as your opportunity to be bad yourself. Instead, live a completely honorable life, because the world is watching. If at all possible, live at peace with everyone. This won't always work. Some people will hate you no matter what. But that's not your concern. Never seek revenge; God has your back. One day he will exalt you and judge them. But today, your job is to show them the utmost respect. So if your opponent is hungry, feed him. If he's is thirsty, give him drink. In every way you would wish to be loved, demonstrate tangible love to your enemies. And if at the end they still want to be your enemy and God's, then he'll deal with it. Don't let their evil overtake you. You overwhelm them with good.

---

27 We typically quote Rom. 12:15 as referring to how believers relate one with another. However, some commentators, including Chrysostom, understand the command to rejoice and mourn along with others to include our disposition toward nonbelievers—even our persecutors. According to Dunn, while this verse addresses Christian behavior in the believing community, Paul did not envision a distinction in "attitudes and obligations—one to fellow believers, the other to nonbelievers." Dunn, *Romans 9–16*, 756.

Clearly this isn't how we typically treat our opponents. Yet this is the kind of gentle respect and dignity we should display to all rulers and authorities, all races and religions, all classes and persuasions, showing due honor to fellow image-bearers. And this shouldn't be that hard. For if we struggle now to do this with a transgender neighbor or a coworker from Saudi Arabia, how are we going to be gracious and bless those who overtly persecute us one day?

To be sure, this is an incredibly high calling. Honoring others doesn't come naturally to us, much less blessing those who seek our harm. However, Christians who are secure in their honor, who have their identity affirmed by God, confer that same dignity on others. They don't have to defend their honor by disrespecting others. They don't have to put others down to prop themselves up.

Instead, by God's grace and his Spirit, we can exalt Christ by respecting others. We can honor our Lord by dignifying our enemies. Not only that, but as we become outcasts in our land, we may gain a greater heart for reaching the least and the lost among us, for showing mercy to the despised and the lonely. The church may rediscover what it looks like to take the gospel, like Jesus, to those on the fringes of society—because we'll be right there with them.

A total role reversal is happening in our nation. Christians used to be respected in society. Churches were revered institutions. Serving as clergy was a noble profession. As such, we could leverage that status to our evangelistic benefit. We could invite people to church and assume they might want to come. We could host evangelistic events with well-known speakers and expect a captive (and large) audience. We could run a summer children's outreach or Sunday school and think even pagan parents might want their kids to get some religion.

But our secular world is increasingly suspicious of religion. Christians are no longer part of the solution; we're the problem. Pastors aren't trustworthy. Churches are suspect. Bible-believers are bigots. Thus the days of attractional evangelism are waning. The times of relying on the gravitational pull of our social standing to bring people into church, a Christian camp, or a revival meeting are all but gone. The time is coming, and is here now, when the world won't listen to our gospel simply because they respect us.

However, they might listen *if we respect them*.

Because how can we expect homosexuals to believe our concern for God's created order when we don't dignify them as people made in his image? How can we call our coworkers to submit to Christ as Lord when they don't see us gladly and respectfully submitting to our boss? How can we tell of God's love for the world when we exhibit disdain and revulsion toward our neighbors? How can we demonstrate a Christ-like compassion for our enemies when all they hear from us is concern for our rights and privileges?

To honor others is to have a genuine care and concern for them. So this is what we must do—even for those who have no concern for us.

SHOWING GENUINE CONCERN

One of the most practical ways we can demonstrate such

concern is through prayer. Even during our exile we can bless the world by praying for *and with* others.[28] This is something I've learned by watching our faithful brothers and sisters all over the world. Everywhere I go I see national believers using prayer as a means to reach out to those around them with love and the gospel.

Praying with and caring for Muslim refugees fleeing war-ravaged Syria. Praying over the demon possessed outside a Bible school in Tanzania. Praying with and blessing English students in Hungary. Praying with fearful earthquake victims suffering in Turkey. Praying over non-Christian parents and children during an Ethiopian coffee ceremony. And praying for impoverished and lonely villagers along the Ukraine-Romania border.

In that last case, Pastor Sorin was my example. As February snowflakes fluttered in the soft wind, Sorin and I traveled together along the rolling Tisza River. The black water flowed past frozen banks and under a sky of white marble. It had been an abnormally cold winter, so we were there delivering care packages to widows on behalf of his church.

Whenever he pulled his small Volkswagen station wagon to stop at a given house, we'd hop out and trudge through mud and snow to bring donated foodstuffs to their door. Invariably the widows would invite us in to warm ourselves by their ceramic tiled stoves. There we'd huddle around as Sorin explained our purpose. We'd come to bless them, sent by the love of Christ and representing his church. Sorin would

---

28 Jeremiah called for Jewish exiles in corrupt Babylon to "seek the welfare of the city" where God had sent them and "pray to the Lord on its behalf" (Jer. 29:7).

take that opportunity to speak briefly, though boldly, of the gospel. Then he'd ask if they had any requests for prayer. After listening to them share about their family, health, and various struggles, we'd each take turns saying grace over our widowed hosts.

As I've observed, nothing demonstrates gentleness and respect quite like praying for someone else in their presence. It shows care for them. It honors them. In doing so we bless rather than curse. Actually, whenever we pray with unbelievers, we have the dual opportunity to honor them and present the good news. In fact, I think sometimes the best ice-breaker for an evangelistic conversation is to pray. When you don't know what else to say you can always ask the question, "Can I pray for you?", then do it right there with them.

In 2 Kings 5 we have the brief account of a young servant girl living in exile who showed concern for and blessed her captors. We know little about her; we're not even given her name. All we know is that Syrian invaders (with God's help) had raided Israel and taken her captive. She ended up far from home, away from family, living as a servant in the home of Naaman, the commander of the Syrian army—her enemy. And this mighty man of valor was afflicted with leprosy.

If we were to put ourselves in her position, what might we do? Most of us have never experienced physical exile. Most of us have never experienced the loss of family, status, or home. Most of us have never lived as a slave. But we might imagine how she could've responded.

She could've loathed the day Naaman's army took her captive, blaming him for her pain. She could've been overwhelmed by grief, dwelling on all she lost. She could've easily been motivated by revenge, interpreting Naaman's suffering as God's just judgment, and been glad. She could've cursed him to his grave.

Instead, she blessed him. She honored her godless master by being concerned for him—concerned enough to open her mouth to his wife. That act alone likely involved a significant measure of risk. How dare a lowly Middle Eastern slave girl give counsel to her mistress and speak on behalf of God! What might have happened to her if Elisha didn't come through and heal Naaman's disease?

But this is exactly what we're called to do as Christian evangelists. In humility and respect, we show genuine concern for our opponents, even those responsible for our exile. We do so because we seek their good more than we seek our rights. We live with respect for all because we desire all to be saved.

This is how Aisha lived for more than a decade, enduring exile in a relationship that took far more than it gave. But through it all she embodied the instruction Peter gave to godly women living as strangers in their own homes. And God blessed her for it.

Some years after our first meeting in her city, our family now back in the states, I received another WhatsApp message on my phone. It was Metin. He rejoiced to tell me he had confessed Christ as Lord. His one request to me: "Can you send someone to our city so I can be baptized?" Today, two years later, I still receive messages from Metin, only now with pictures from the small church gathering in their home.

DECLARING HIS PRAISES

"BUT YOU ARE A CHOSEN RACE, A ROYAL PRIESTHOOD, A HOLY NATION, A PEOPLE FOR HIS OWN POSSESSION, THAT YOU MAY PROCLAIM THE EXCELLENCIES OF HIM WHO CALLED YOU OUT OF DARKNESS INTO HIS MARVELOUS LIGHT. ONCE YOU WERE NOT A PEOPLE, BUT NOW YOU ARE GOD'S PEOPLE; ONCE YOU HAD NOT RECEIVED MERCY, BUT NOW YOU HAVE RECEIVED MERCY."

—PETER THE APOSTLE (1 PET. 2:9-10)

Meryem is a spunky young woman with full, dark chocolate eyes and even darker hair. At 17 years old, she was everything you'd expect from a teenaged girl, but with a steadfast passion for the gospel. Only a few months into her newfound faith, Meryem was already an ardent evangelist, regularly reporting to me about witnessing opportunities with classmates and friends. I remember one such occasion in particular.

It was late afternoon, and a text came to my phone. Meryem was asking me to pray. The principal of her school had called her into his office because of Meryem's outspoken faith. He was threatening her with expulsion, with public shaming, even the possibility of reporting her to a local prosecutor on charges of "missionary activity."

Meryem's run-in with the administrator began earlier that day through an interaction with her teacher. He had been lecturing on Christianity, explaining that Christians believe in three different gods, that they are guilty of *shirk* (the worst possible sin in Islam) by worshiping Jesus, and that they accept four different *incil* (or Gospels) that are corrupt and contradictory. The lecture was one he had likely repeated many times, and it's doubtful he ever encountered pushback.

But on that day, at some point in his lesson, Meryem raised her hand. She asked if she could amend his description, explaining that Christians didn't believe exactly as he suggested. The teacher, taken aback, then asked with impertinence, "How would you know?" In reply, Meryem revealed she had actually read the Bible—she even had one with her!

So before a classroom of 38 students and in a high school without a single other Christian, Meryem boldly defended the gospel. She asserted that Christians believe in only one God. She clarified that the four Gospels demonstrate a unified message of how Jesus is the Christ: the Messiah who fulfills all the Old Testament promises (from prophets Muslims claim to accept). She even began to describe how she came to find certain Islamic understandings to be unconvincing and untenable. But before she could reason further, the teacher abruptly stopped her.

When I learned how courageous Meryem had been, I was curious what led her to take such a stand. After all, she must have anticipated the negative consequences from speaking so openly about her faith in front of her peers, not to mention the culturally unthinkable action of correcting her instructor.

What Meryem told me, though, was that in the moment

she was simply overcome with the sense that her friends were following falsehoods. They were misinformed about Christianity. And what bothered her most was that they were blindly accepting the opinions of others without all the facts. So her growing desire—not just at that moment, but ever since her conversion—was to find a way to explain the gospel to them. As Meryem later told me, she had been "waiting for an opportunity" like this for some time. She had to take it.

WAITING FOR GOSPEL OPPORTUNITIES

I imagine that many of us are like Meryem. We're grieved by the lies others believe about Christ or even about us. We're concerned for them to know the truth. We want them to experience the same life and forgiveness we've found in him. Many of us are, also just like her, waiting for the perfect opportunity to clarify our faith and tell others the good news.

But I think there's a striking difference between many of us and Meryem. Put in her position I doubt we'd have assessed the situation as an opportunity from the Lord. And most likely we wouldn't have acted on it. That's because we increasingly define "evangelistic opportunities" as those rare instances where we perceive others to be open to the gospel. When we think we have a willing audience. When we surmise that those around us are sympathetic to our perspective and will listen without rebuttal.

As we come to Peter's first epistle, we may even assume that he advocated for such a passive witness. That when we live as exiles, we ultimately rely on silent testimony. That we merely depend on others observing a living hope in us, then asking us to tell them about it. That we should delay our witness, sometimes for years, waiting for opportunities like we'd wait for a nibble on a fishing line.[29]

But Peter never intended to portray our evangelism as exiles solely in terms of quiet humility and respectable conduct. He expected Christians facing shame and social exclusion to embrace their exile by boldly preaching the gospel with authority—even when others don't want to hear it.[30] Even when such proclamation is sure to invite ridicule and suffering.

In fact, Peter framed his readers' responsibility to preach the gospel in view of their own rejection. Writing to those who were suffering like Christ, as stones rejected like the chief cornerstone, he encouraged them with their unique status as a spiritual house and holy priesthood, ones chosen by God to offer spiritual sacrifices (2:5).[31] As a kingdom of priests, their calling was to "proclaim the excellencies" of him who delivered them "out of darkness into his marvelous light" (2:10).

---

29 For Jesus's disciples the call to be "fishers of men" didn't conjure images of a leisurely weekend on the shore passively waiting for a bite. They understood fishing to be labor. It involved risk and implied a proactive approach of launching out with nets to claim a catch.

30 When Paul reflected on his own evangelistic ministry in Ephesus, he said that it was marked by both humility and a bold declaration of the gospel (Acts 20:18–21).

31 Peter's reference to the priestly responsibility of offering spiritual sacrifices is a reflection on Isa. 56:7. Paul also linked his own missionary efforts of preaching the gospel to Isa. 66:18–20, with his priestly "offering" referring to Gentiles who believe (Rom. 15:16). For more discussion on Peter's framing of the church's mission in terms of Israel's role as a light to the nations, as well as Paul's understanding of his priestly responsibility to preach the gospel, see Kostenberger and O'Brien, *Salvation to the Ends of the Earth* (Downers Grove, IL: IVP, 2001).

But proclamation of any kind can be especially difficult as exiles. After all, we're not in a position of authority, so how can we speak with it? And isn't authoritative speech unnecessarily offensive?

So we often passively wait for gospel opportunities. We submit the call of the Great Commission to the will of those ill-disposed to our message. We defer preaching to suitable situations—or just the pulpit. We placate others by hemming and hawing about our convictions or their sin. Or we avoid awkward religious conversations altogether.

Perhaps in the past we could get by with such a hands-off approach, when we could count on a reasonable percentage of the population having a favorable view of the church. But depending entirely on others to express interest in our gospel is less tenable as society becomes increasingly disillusioned by our faith, and we become an excluded minority.

If we continue the pattern of waiting for perfect opportunities, they may never come. And our fate will be that of the wary farmer who observes the wind and doesn't sow, who considers the clouds and never reaps (Eccles. 11:4). Such farmers have empty barns in winter. We too, if we're too busy trying to discern the times, raising a moistened finger to the wind to see if someone is ready to respond to the gospel, will likely never see a harvest of souls. We'll never open our mouths to speak, because we'll be waiting for a better day. But better days don't seem to be on the horizon.

RESETTING EXPECTATIONS

Mustafa is a 22-year-old believer from Central Asia. Before he was even a teenager, his conservative parents enrolled him in a Muslim theological training school much like a *madrasa*. From a young age, the trajectory of his life was to become an *imam*, to serve as a religious leader in Islam.

But at some point in his education, Mustafa came into possession of a New Testament. He began investigating it intently. As a student he had already read the Qur'an and found it less than conclusive. Whenever he had approached his Islamic instructors about questions or inconsistencies, they deflected, discouraging him from further inquiry. But this failed to satiate his curiosity. So when he began to encounter the text of the Bible, he was eager to learn as much as he could. And for the first time, as he explains it, while pouring over its pages, he experienced profound peace.

About a year later, through his ongoing study, Mustafa came to faith in Christ, basically independent of any outside influence. In fact, his relative isolation continued throughout his high school years and young adult life. As my friend who now disciples him describes it, Mustafa's growth in grace and knowledge was something like that of Saul in the New Testament. He was converted to Christ and didn't immediately consult with others. As such, the Bible became the primary influence for his understanding of the Christian life.

Just two weeks ago my friend was leading a discipleship study with Mustafa and a few other believers who come from the same unreached people group. Toward the end of the meeting they began to discuss evangelism. That's when other believers in the room started repeating platitudes to endorse a hesitant, if not passive, approach: "You have to pick your spots," and "It's not always appropriate to share."

As their conversation gathered steam, they continued to suggest all manner of considerations that must be made before a former Muslim should ever broach the subject of Christ with family or friends.

Meanwhile, Mustafa sat silently, his hands folded across the small New Testament on his lap. His eyes betrayed an active mind. My friend, sensing Mustafa might have something to contribute, invited him to enter the conversation.

Gently leaning forward in his chair, Mustafa quietly shared wisdom beyond his years. He explained that prior to talking with someone about the gospel, he starts by resetting his expectations. He does this by rehearsing passages where Jesus explains exactly what will happen to his followers when they speak for him. "We're going to be insulted," he said. "Jesus promised we'll be ostracized and maybe even beaten. So I set my expectations according to his Word," he continued, "that way I'm not surprised when something bad happens."

Mustafa explained that once he's adjusted his perspective, he prays for boldness. Only then does he feel ready to be a witness. Looking around the small room he concluded, "Believe me, brothers, I've been ostracized and insulted. But I've received a blessing from the Lord every time I've opened my mouth."

As my friend relayed this short story to me about Mustafa's courage, he admitted that—perhaps in his own lack of faith—he's come to refer to Mustafa as a unicorn. So many young Central Asians that we've discipled over the years are overwhelmed by fears (often genuine) and silenced by shame. They don't want to suffer or be killed. They don't want to lose their job. Perhaps most significant of all, they don't want to be abandoned or excluded by their families.

In fact, Mustafa himself has experienced this. When his family eventually came to the realization that he wasn't just going through a phase, that he wasn't just dabbling in religion, and that he had actually chosen to follow Christ, they reacted strongly. His father refused to speak with him. His brothers tried to convince him to turn back. His mother called to urge him to reconsider. Weeping on the other end of the line she pleaded, "Be a thief. Be a drug dealer. Be a liar. But please," she begged, "don't be a Christian!"

PROBLEM WITH MERELY 'SHARING THE GOSPEL'

For some time now, American Christians have conceived of their witness in terms of "sharing the gospel." Read any book or listen to any talk on personal evangelism and you'll inevitably encounter the phrase. On one level, the terminology is positive, conveying the gracious act of giving others a treasure we possess. However, if by "sharing" we imply a kind of charity where we only give the gospel to willing recipients, then our Christian vernacular has become a problem. Especially since the Bible rarely uses such language to describe the act of evangelism.[32]

I first awakened to this reality while doing language study

---

32 One possible exception would be 1 Thess. 2:8, though the idea of "sharing" in that context is filled out by descriptive verbs that connote authoritative proclamation (such as declaring, exhorting, and charging) in the context of compassion and gentleness (like a nursing mother).

in Central Asia. As I took a course in spiritual terminology, a missionary teacher bemoaned the fact that many Westerners had imported the idea of sharing the gospel into the vocabulary of the local church. He asserted that such a concept was completely foreign—to their context and the Bible. Scripture, instead, spoke primarily of preaching the gospel, declaring and proclaiming a message.

But what, you might ask, could be wrong with *sharing* the gospel? Isn't the greater problem that people aren't sharing it at all? However, I've come to wonder if these dual realities aren't somehow related, with the way we speak *about* evangelism imperceptibly affecting the way we *do* evangelism.

Throughout the book of Acts we find repeated examples of authoritative witness—even in the face of suffering—from the apostles and early church. We find them proclaiming the gospel and speaking boldly. We read of them persuading others. We see them reasoning from Scripture, both expounding and also applying it. We observe them testifying before rulers and governors, bearing witness before civil crowds and angry mobs. What we don't find them doing is "sharing" the gospel.

So it's more than a bit curious that the dominant way American Christians describe the act of evangelism is in terms of sharing. This isn't just one way we talk about it; it's almost the only way we talk about it. And I believe this lack of clarity is more than an issue of semantics.

It would be no different from a baseball coach who consistently described the role of pitchers in terms of *tossing* the ball. In practice or a game, whenever his pitchers were struggling to get batters out, what if his dominant instruction was simply to *toss* the ball? Not throw strikes. Not work the corners. Not change speeds. Not pound it inside. Just toss the ball. Would the pitchers have an accurate understanding of their responsibility?

But that's basically the way we talk about evangelism. Our description is overly simplistic. It lacks precision and nuance. And when that becomes our default instruction—to simply *share the gospel*—we fail to convey the attitude, approach, and authority necessary for the act itself. Thus what started as a subtle change in terminology results in a massive shift in our whole ethos of evangelism.

That's because "sharing" typically involves the act of giving something to someone who desires it. Children share (or don't share) Legos with other kids who want them. Friends share a great cookie recipe with another friend who asks for it. Or we might share money with those holding a cardboard sign at the street corner. In each case, we share with others because they're asking for what we possess. But the reality is, few people are ever begging us to share the gospel with them.

We must ask ourselves, then, whether casual Christianese has influenced the way we view the gospel mandate. We must consider why we're only willing to speak the gospel when we perceive openness on the part of another. We must ponder whether we even have a category for proclaiming a message that people oppose, one that's innately offensive. Or do we tiptoe through polite spiritual conversations and timidly share our opinions, then call it evangelism?

But to evangelize is *to preach good news*. According to D. A. Carson, this is the basic definition of the Greek word *euangelizo* from which we get our English word for evangelism. As he observes in his comprehensive study of the "gospel" word-group in the Bible, "the gospel is primarily displayed in heraldic proclamation: the gospel is announced, proclaimed, preached, precisely because it is God's spectacular news."[33] In fact, Carson expresses concern that some of our confusion (what he labels as "nonsense") about what the gospel is (and how it must be communicated) results from our lack of understanding regarding how the Bible describes the gospel and evangelism in the first place.[34]

Far more than just sharing, evangelism involves testifying to Christ—warning, persuading, defending, pleading, and calling. As we saw last chapter, such authoritative witness need not be in opposition to gentleness and respect. Moreover, the context of healthy, trusting relationships can actually add force to our words. But sadly we often value those relationships more than a clear statement of the truth. Rarely do we engage people with a sense of authority or urgency.

URGENCY OF OUR MESSAGE

Last year I had the privilege of teaching the letter of 2 Timothy

---

33 Carson explains further, "The essentially heraldic element in preaching is bound up with the fact that the core message is not a code of ethics to be debated, still less a list of aphorisms to be admired and pondered, and certainly not a systematic theology to be outlined and schematized. Though it properly grounds ethics, aphorisms, and systematics, it is none of these three: it is news, good news, and therefore must be publicly announced." D. A. Carson "What is the Gospel?—Revisited," in *For the Fame of God's Name*, eds. by Sam Storms and Justin Taylor (Wheaton: Crossway, 2010), 158.

34 Carson, "What Is the Gospel?—Revisited," 155.

to church leaders in South Asia—their final course in a three-year program. Our focus was Paul's exhortation to faithfully preach the good news, a particularly appropriate lesson for graduating pastors. Throughout the week I reminded them of Paul's farewell to his young apprentice, encouraging Timothy not to be ashamed of the testimony of the Lord, but rather to embrace suffering and persecution—like Paul and Christ—for the sake of the gospel (2 Tim. 1:9).[35]

Less than a week later, as I sat in my home, a story popped up in my news feed from the same South Asian country. The headline read that Christian conversion and evangelism were now banned. Suddenly, the previous week's teaching took on greater significance.

In such situations, some might sympathize with those South Asian leaders and encourage them to avoid confrontation. Better to lay low and maintain your presence in the community. Better to remain quiet so you can provide for your family. Better to witness to others through your good reputation. But that's not what the apostles practiced (Acts 4:20), and it's not how Paul charged Timothy. So with a grieving concern for my students I prayed they wouldn't be ashamed of the gospel but would boldly fulfill their ministry, doing the work of an evangelist.

One of the clearest biblical examples of doing evangelism as an exile actually comes from an Old Testament figure, Noah.[36] Noah lived as a lonely outcast, warning others of the wrath

---

35 See more of Paul's example and exhortation to this end in 2 Tim. 2:8–10; 4:1–5.

36 Granted, the references to Noah in Peter are less than clear, but Noah's stark situation obviously mirrored that of Peter's readers, and Peter saw him as a model preacher.

to come. It makes sense then that Peter would repeatedly refer to the days of Noah as he wrote to Christians living as strangers in their own land. Specifically, Peter referenced Noah as being a *herald* of righteousness (2 Pet. 2:5). Through him Christ *preached* to those who were disobedient (3:19).

These mentions of Noah's ministry of proclamation are admittedly ambiguous (and Peter thought Paul was hard to understand!). But it seems reasonable that Noah would be the perfect reference point for Christian exiles in first-century Asia. Peter had called them to faithfully declare with authority the praises of Jesus. And Noah's experience as a forsaken preacher would've easily resonated with them—because news of an executed Jew from the Galilean backwater now establishing a kingdom of priests from every nation sounds just about as believable as forecasts of an impending and catastrophic flood on a cloudless day in Mesopotamia.

But Noah's story had at least one more correlation to Peter's readers. Jesus said that the coming of the Son of Man would be like the days of Noah (Matt. 24:36–40). Just as people in Noah's day were eating, drinking, and going about their normal lives until they were suddenly swept away by the flood, so it will be at the coming of Christ. Judgment will come swiftly, when least expected. This coming judgment, Peter emphasized, is why the gospel must be proclaimed (4:6). It's why we must announce it with urgency, even to those who deride our message and mock our faith. Even when it involves risk.

Meryem was a unique case of an unbeliever actually asking us to explain the gospel to her. When we first met, I was standing outside of a clothing store in a shopping mall waiting for my wife. We'd gone there expressly to connect with Meryem because she had requested a copy of the Bible. However, when she didn't show up, my wife ducked into the nearby store.

Minutes later, though, a short and spirited girl walked up and introduced herself. It was Meryem. The only problem was that I was expecting someone much older, not this baby-faced teenager staring up at me. I was immediately concerned.

This wasn't my first time setting up a blind rendezvous to deliver a Bible. Those curious about Christianity in our country could request a free copy advertised on various media (newspaper ads, Facebook pages, Google ads, and traditional websites). Whenever those requests came from our city, I was responsible for setting up a meeting. But since I never knew who would come (police, extremists, or genuine seekers), I generally preferred a public gathering spot like a park or shopping mall. Thankfully, until that day, I never had any real issues.

But Meryem presented a dilemma. She was clearly a minor. And in our Central Asian country, it was illegal to proselytize anyone younger than 18. So as we stood at the mall's entrance exchanging greetings and initial niceties, I stalled, waiting for my wife to exit the clothing store and help me navigate the situation.

When she did, we made our way outside and across the street to the park. We sat down to tea and juice, then asked Meryem about her family, her interest in the Bible, and ultimately her age. When she revealed that she was only 17, I explained our difficult situation.

We couldn't give her a Bible. We weren't allowed to influence her in any way to Christianity. The result could be expulsion from the country, or worse. We told her we first would need the permission of her parents. But Meryem wouldn't take no for an answer. She pressed us to speak with her then and there. "What if my mom doesn't allow it?" she asked. "And how am I going to learn this stuff? I don't know any Christians."[37]

As she continued to make her case, my wife and I looked at each other knowingly, sensing the urgency of the situation. *This is why we had come to this country. This is why we left everything. If there were ever a time to risk everything, this had to be it. After all, were we really going to wait a whole year to explain the gospel to her? The time was now.* So as Meryem's plea came to an end, I reached into my backpack and pulled out a Bible. Then together we reasoned with her about the good news of Jesus—news she had never before heard from anyone's lips.[38]

PRAISE: THE CONTENT OF OUR PROCLAMATION

When we think about speaking the gospel with urgency and authority, we may envision a fiery preacher pounding a pulpit, or perhaps a man in a sandwich board warning of judgment

---

37 This was truly a rare instance. In this chapter I'm not arguing that people never inquire about the gospel—Peter says they will. But we can't be entirely dependent on such interest.

38 Within the week we set up a meeting with Meryem's mother as a way to show honor to her and to the law. Over the course of the next couple years, we met repeatedly with both of them to discuss the Bible. Within months, Meryem believed and was baptized. Three years later, her mother was as well.

to passersby. But that day, sitting on plastic chairs in the park, I just tried to explain to Meryem how Jesus is good news for us—and for the world. I wanted her to understand the joy and forgiveness he brings to our lives. The urgency of the moment opened my mouth with praise, not with stormy rhetoric.

Likewise, Peter described the content of our exilic proclamation as praise. He called us as priests to declare God's glory to others. Yes, we preach Christ crucified. But we do so glorying in the cross. We exult in God, and our adulation overflows to others, telling them how he has delivered us from darkness and into glorious light. In other words, worship is essential to evangelism.

These days we tend to view preaching as something only preachers do. But preaching is really a close cousin to praise—and we praise things all the time. As C. S. Lewis observed, we praise that which we most enjoy. In fact, our enjoyment of something isn't complete until we have communicated that happiness to others. So joy—in a good book or a breathtaking vista—finds its fullness in the expression of praise, in declaring our experience to others so they too can share in it.[39]

This kind of effervescent witness is actually God's design for his people all along. Israel had been called out from among the nations to be a kingdom of priests and a holy nation (Ex. 19:6). They were to sing to the Lord and declare his glory among the peoples (1 Chron. 16:23–24). Now God has

---

[39] From C. S. Lewis, *Reflections on the Psalms* (New York: Harcourt, Brace and Company, 1958), 95.

conferred on us—Jew and Gentile believers in Jesus—this priestly ministry. Simply put, God saved us to praise him.

Peter tells us we've been set apart for this special service. We're called to declare God's praises to the world. So if we're not faithfully proclaiming the gospel to those around us, it's owing to the fact we're not overflowing in praise to God. If evangelism doesn't exist, it's because worship doesn't.[40]

Praise is the most natural thing in the world for us, and we do it all the time. We brag about our favorite sports team. We rave about restaurants. We shamelessly tell others about the deals we find online. We can't stop talking about the latest Netflix series or our last vacation. We adore musicians, endorse politicians, and fawn over celebrities. We promote our kids' school and post about our morning coffee. We sing the praises of just about everything, even gluten-free pizza.

But ask us to raise our voices in praise to God outside of weekend worship, and we struggle to string together a whole sentence. While we (I include myself here) demonstrate an incredible ability to proclaim the glories of endless earthly trivialities, we somehow stutter and stammer at the opportunity to speak with others about our heavenly hope. So it's obvious our gospel silence isn't because our mouths are broken; it's because our hearts are. Because if we worshiped God as we should, our neighbors, coworkers, and friends would be the first to hear about it.

---

40 John Piper famously wrote, "Missions exists because worship doesn't." Piper, *Let the Nations Be Glad* (Grand Rapids: Baker, 1993), 11. But Piper does more than suggest that worship is the goal of missions. He also asserts that worship is the fuel of the missionary endeavor. This is the sense that I am emphasizing, suggesting that our lack of evangelism is the byproduct of weak worship.

This reality may bring us some needed humiliation. But we should also recognize the incredible untapped resource of praise for our mission as exiles. Because, as we've already seen from the Philippian jailhouse, praise has amazing power coming from an outcast. Just ask the Samaritan at the well.

She was an immoral woman, likely ashamed of her own shadow, coming to the community well in the heat of the day when no one else would be around. Except on that particular day a stranger was waiting for her. Jesus then initiated a culturally unthinkable conversation with this Samaritan as a way to introduce her to living water. Through the course of their encounter, he revealed himself as Messiah and uncovered her secret sins. In response, she ran to the townspeople (her shame suddenly vanished) to proclaim to them, "Come, see a man who told me all that I ever did. Can this be the Christ?" (John 4:29). And many believed.

In her story we see how coming face-to-face with Jesus has a way of overpowering the shame that silences us. Whereas shame and social exclusion tend to push us away from engaging others, a personal encounter with the Lord transforms our hearts in worship and sends us running to others in praise of Jesus—even to the very people who made us outcasts in the first place.

DECLARING THE GOSPEL TO OTHERS

As this chapter draws to a close, I want to conclude with three practical suggestions for how to grow in declaring God's praises. I tried to implement these three principles while living overseas in an effort to communicate authority, urgency, and worship in my own evangelism.

1. BE WILLING TO OFFEND (AUTHORITY)

If you proclaim the gospel, it will be offensive—there's no way around it. There will be inevitable conflict. You must come to a point of being willing to offend, or else you'll never say much of anything. Part of my attempt to do this in a Muslim nation was to make unexpected and provocative statements about my faith. The goal wasn't to offend but to get them thinking.

For instance, when someone would ask whether or not I believed Jesus to be God's Son—a concept extremely offensive to Muslims—I'd answer in the affirmative. But then I'd push it one step further: "Christians don't just believe he's God's Son, they believe Jesus *is God!*" I'd take them to John 1:3 and show that he was creator of all—even all the prophets.

Often they would ask if I accepted their prophet or holy book. At first I dreaded that potential minefield. But I came to appreciate the opportunity to tell them that, as a Christian, there's no way I could in good conscience. Because I believe the Bible, and it says a Christian can't accept another gospel—even if it comes from an angel. I would show them from Galatians 1:8 that anyone who propagates any different message is under God's curse.[41]

---

41 Gal. 1:8 presents a significant biblical case against Islam, especially since Qur'anic revelation is said to have come through the angel Gabriel.

One common rebuttal I would receive was, "We believe in Jesus too. He's one of our prophets." In response, I'd suggest that Jesus made for a miserable prophet. Prophets of Allah should show the way and teach the truth. But Jesus said, "*I am* the way; *I am* the truth."[42] Then I'd add, "Sounds like blasphemy, don't you think?"

This was perhaps the approach I would use the most: demonstrating the foolishness of the gospel—and my own foolishness for believing it—if it wasn't true. Such a rhetorical device comes straight from Paul, who argued that we're most to be pitied if the resurrection is a lie (1 Cor. 15:19) and that Jesus's death was a waste if we could attain our own righteousness (Gal. 2:21). Such provocative statements demonstrated I'd thought through the ramifications of my beliefs. *What if I'm wrong?* But it also enabled me to press upon them: "What if you're wrong?"

2. CALL FOR A RESPONSE (URGENCY)

About halfway into my time overseas I became convicted that I rarely challenged people to repent and believe the gospel. I could argue for the deity of Christ. I might reason with them about Scripture's truthfulness. I could try to persuade them about the need for God's justice against sin. I might even speak boldly about the cross and resurrection. But I wasn't closing the argument with a sense of urgency. I wasn't calling for a response.

Actually, it was about the time we met Meryem that I began to change my approach. I realized that evangelism wasn't

---

42 I'm indebted to a national believer for this simple argument from John 14:6.

simply engaging in religious dialogue and exchanging ideas. The gospel was a summons. God commands all people everywhere to repent, and he uses human preachers to do so. It wasn't enough to simply tell others what *I* believed to be true; I had to tell them what *they* needed to do.

Of course, such a posture conveys urgency. But it also demonstrates love. Because, when you plead with others to turn from sin, sometimes you do so with tears. When you warn friends sitting at your dining table about coming judgment, you get a lump in your throat. You don't do so flippantly, but compassionately. You call them to join you in following Jesus. You invite them to believe the glorious good news.

3. DELIGHT IN THE GOSPEL (WORSHIP)

We must recognize that the apologetic force of our preaching isn't always that our message is more believable than another, but that it's more desirable. In evangelism, we don't simply make a logical case, but a doxological one. We aren't just talking to brains. We're speaking to hearts that have desires and eyes that look for beauty. We're not merely trying to convince people that our gospel is true, but that our God is good.

Over the years I've tried to move away from cold, structured arguments into exultations of praise. From giving evidence for the resurrection to reveling in its glory. From merely explaining why Jesus is needed to showing why he should be wanted. From defending the Bible's truthfulness to rejoicing in its sweetness.

Preaching the gospel requires propositional truths. Believing the gospel requires historical facts. But when we preach, others should *see* how those facts have changed our lives. They should *hear* us singing with the Negro slaves, "I've found a Savior, and he's sweet, I know." They need to *feel* the weight of glory. That's because believing the gospel—like preaching it—is worship. Which makes praise integral to our preaching and turns our priestly ministry into delight!

CHAPTER 5

VISIBLY

DIFFERENT

"BELOVED, I URGE YOU AS
SOJOURNERS AND EXILES TO
ABSTAIN FROM THE PASSIONS OF THE
FLESH, WHICH WAGE WAR AGAINST
YOUR SOUL. KEEP YOUR CONDUCT
AMONG THE GENTILES HONORABLE,
SO THAT WHEN THEY SPEAK AGAINST
YOU AS EVILDOERS, THEY MAY SEE
YOUR GOOD DEEDS AND GLORIFY
GOD ON THE DAY OF VISITATION."

—PETER THE APOSTLE (1 PET. 2:11-12)

My wife's close friendship with our next-door neighbor developed on the floor of her two-bedroom apartment. It was actually common for women to gather on the floor in our building, where they sat on kitchen rugs or scattered cushions sharing endless glasses of tea, passing the daily gossip or trading marital advice. But that's not how this particular friendship deepened. Theirs intensified when my wife was sprawled out on the neighbor's laminate entryway, her head in the arms of Asmin.

Asmin was a mother of three and a nurse at the nearby state-run hospital. My wife, meanwhile, had been struggling with significant health issues for a number of years. Occasionally when I was traveling for work or away from home, she would end up needing urgent care. So having Asmin across the hall was like having a walk-in clinic in your backyard—without a waiting room!

Over time as she came to depend more and more on Asmin, the friendship between both families grew. Our kids spent summer days outside together. On long winter weekends, Asmin's children came over to our house to play games, do puzzles, or color pages. I taught their daughter some English. Her dad taught my son chess. They'd have our family over in the evening for fruit and cakes, and we'd be sure to visit them on their Muslim holidays. But throughout our families' burgeoning kinship, my wife's bond with Asmin remained the strongest.

As they spent increased time together, my wife would often look for ways to speak to Asmin about faith in Christ. She reasoned with her from the Scriptures and gave her a copy of the Bible in her language. For a while, Asmin even began to read it—perhaps out of interest, perhaps only curiosity. One December, she came to our apartment to observe our Christmas traditions. She walked through our home like an art gallery, taking pictures of our Advent calendar and decorations. Her plan was to show the photographs around the hospital to her coworkers. We had become a spectacle.

One day, when my wife had to go to the hospital for some tests, Asmin invited her to the urology floor where she was on duty. They met at the nurses' station, then Asmin invited her into the break room. There in a small room, huddled around an old television as curls of cigarette smoke exited an open window, a cadre of nurses sought respite from their rounds—or perhaps they were there for the coming show.

Asmin introduced my wife as her American neighbor and friend, and as a Christian. However, she quickly gave one important caveat: "Not the kind of Christian you think." As doctors and orderlies peeked in the door, she explained how our family was honorable and kind. How my wife and daughters dressed modestly. How I was faithful in our marriage. How we were clean and considerate. We were Christians, yes; but we were actually people of good character. We were neighbors they could trust.

BE WHO GOD IS

The twin themes of goodness and godliness pervade the epistle of 1 Peter. The apostle greets exiled readers as those who have been *set apart* by the Spirit *to obey* Jesus Christ (1:2). He then praises the Father for causing them to be born again to a living hope through Jesus's resurrection. Throughout the rest of the letter he continues to encourage these suffering believers with that eternal outlook while also challenging them to live in present, visible holiness.

In fact, their hope in future grace at Christ's return was to lead them to a transformed life of obedience (1:13–14). As John writes in his first epistle, the Christian hope of glory is one significant reason why we purify ourselves just as God is pure (1 John 3:3). Likewise, Peter calls his readers to be holy as their heavenly Father is holy (1:15). Then, in the next breath—in case they didn't catch it the first time—he repeats the command, citing the words of Yahweh to Israel in the old covenant: "You shall be holy, for I am holy" (1:16).

As we saw in the last chapter, the believing community in first-century Asia was to see their experience as mirroring Israel's. God had chosen and called them out from among the nations to be his holy and peculiar people. He had set them apart as a visible demonstration of his own holiness, to be shining lights in the world. As an assembly of priests in God's kingdom, they were to mediate God's presence and radiate his glory. But in order to do so, they needed to be like their King. So too, believers within the new covenant have this great commission: to be holy as God is holy. We're to be who he is.

Today, the mantra of American culture is to "be who you are." "You do you" is the message. Whether it's a self-help talk show or the latest Disney production, the basic instruction is that we should cast off the chains of others' expectations and desires. Don't let them dictate who you are or what you do with your life. Fulfillment and lasting happiness wait for those who follow their own path, being true to themselves.

In a way, this is exactly the logic of the Bible when it comes to Christian living. We're not to concern ourselves with the world's expectations. We're told to be who we are—that is, who God has made us to be as new creations in Christ. Paul could write to Christians in the corrupt city (and church) of Corinth, addressing them as the sanctified who are called to be saints (1 Cor. 1:2). Or Peter could write to those God had set apart as holy, telling them to actually be holy. Both of them followed the example of Jesus, who instructed his disciples: you are the light of the world, so let your light shine by doing good deeds (Matt. 5:14–16).

However, our new nature isn't the ultimate standard for who we're to be and how we're to live. The fundamental reality behind who we are as Christians is God himself. So Peter calls us to be like God. To be holy as he is holy. Or as John expresses it: to walk in the light as he is in the light.

God himself is light. At conversion he transfers us from the kingdom of darkness to the kingdom of his Son. This isn't a physical relocation (at least not yet), such as moving from Texas to Illinois. This change is positional and ontological. We're made light through his creative act. And now as that light, we're summoned to shine in the world through our good deeds. Then, like Paul's commissioning on the road to Damascus, we're sent out to preach the gospel and open the eyes of the blind so they too might turn from darkness to light (Acts 26:17–18).[43]

Holiness, therefore, is the necessary effect and means of the gospel. In other words, holiness is not only the result of conversion, it's also an embodied argument in support of the gospel's veracity. We're saved to be holy, and we become holy so others will be saved. To use an agricultural analogy, godliness is the fruit of our salvation but also the cultivation of others' salvation. In the gospel we're recreated to be like God so we will then demonstrate who God is to the world.

We know the gospel has many powerful effects on our lives: deliverance from sin, communion with the saints, an eternal inheritance. But another critical and sometimes forgotten outcome of our conversion—and part of the message we proclaim—is that we've been transferred out of darkness and into God's glorious light. As such, an integral part of our evangelism is the visible demonstration of our new nature as those walking in the light. Gospel declaration is linked to life transformation.

---

43 Part of evangelism and discipleship is calling others to follow us as we follow Christ— for them to be who we are (1 Cor. 4:16; 11:1). This is another reason why personal holiness is critical for the evangelist.

DOING GOOD TO BE
SEEN BY OTHERS

In a way, then, personal holiness must precede evangelism. As Peter wrote, we were set apart to be holy priests in order to declare the praises of God. Our behavior and reputation as exiles were of utmost concern to Peter—filling out so much of his letter—because of their inescapable influence on our witness and God's glory. Consequently, Christians who live in sin will inevitably betray the gospel and besmirch God's character.

That organic connection between holiness and evangelism often leaves us hesitant to open our mouths with the gospel. We know people are watching. We're aware that the most common criticism of Christians is that we're hypocrites—that our unholy selves don't always align with our holy book. We also realize that if we dare speak the gospel we'll be inviting greater scrutiny.

We know that when we preach good news to others, we're basically welcoming their critical eye on God's Word based on our own character. We're asking them to consider Christ in view of how we relate to others. We're giving people permission to examine our confession of faith in light of how we handle trials and difficulties. And these concerns stifle our witness, not so much because we know what others will hear from our lips, but because of what they've already seen in our lives. We may not be ashamed of Christ, but we might be ashamed of our noticeable greed, self-pity, anger, gluttony, jealousy, lust, and disrespect.

But I think this is exactly the kind of accountability and

introspection Peter wants to cultivate.[44] The desire to reach others for Christ has a way of encouraging us to greater godliness. Just as we purify ourselves because of a future hope, we clean up our lives—and clean up our mouths—because we want others to believe and be saved. (God has a way of giving us multiple motivations for obedience, probably because he knows we need them.) Peter, therefore, expected his readers to live in such a way that their deeds would be observable to those around them and commendable as righteous and godly, selfless and compassionate. In other words, he wanted us to do good to be seen by others (2:11–12).

That might seem strange for a number of reasons. For one, isn't it terribly arrogant? Isn't our gospel a message of telling people how broken and sinful *we are*? Isn't the church meant to be a hospital for sinners, not a hotel for saints?[45]

Yes, and no. The hospital is only desirable if it's more than a quarantined building where the terminally ill go to die. I've seen my share of dirty hospitals in the world, and you don't want to go there. A hospital is only a good place if there's medicine and a remedy. There must be visible evidence of a cure: we who were once on our deathbeds have found the antidote. Our gospel is for sick sinners, to be sure. But we preach as healed saints, as those who are being delivered from the malignancy of our former corruption.

---

44 I'm not implying here a purely individualistic approach to personal holiness. The New Testament epistles assume a corporate audience and application. So the local church is critical to the pursuit of holiness (through discipleship, accountability, preaching, and prayer). Likewise, the New Testament envisions the power of a collective witness through a transformed body demonstrating love and good deeds in community together.

45 I certainly resonate with the quote referenced here and attributed to Augustine; however, I'm addressing a slightly different issue.

Still we might flinch at the thought of displaying our good deeds before others. After all, Jesus instructed his disciples not to perform acts of worship to be seen by others, because that's what the hypocrites do. However, we sometimes miss how, in the same sermon, Jesus told his followers to let their light shine before others so that they would see their good deeds and give glory to God (Matt. 6:1; 5:16).

One way to resolve these two seemingly opposing ideas in Jesus's teaching is to observe the opposite purpose implicit in each. If we act in ways to draw attention to ourselves and receive others' praise, then we're guilty of the hypocrisy that Jesus condemned. Our reward is complete with them noticing us. However, wanting others to see our good deeds isn't always bad. Such demonstrable works of goodness are admirable if they flow from a pure heart and if our goal is God's glory.

Peter's address to the wives of unbelieving husbands can be instructive here. As we've already discussed, he called them to seek to win their spouses through their respect and pure conduct. Rather than focusing on external adornments such as extravagant jewelry or lavish clothing, they were to ornament their lives with gentleness and holiness. But by comparing their inward disposition and behavior with adornments and accessories, Peter was clearly communicating that their godliness should be noticeable. He wanted their husbands to see their good deeds. Such godliness would commend their gospel.

Having lived in both America and Central Asia, our family has had many discussions about modesty over the years—with our daughters and our son. Since expectations of acceptable clothing change from culture to culture, we often chose to emphasize the importance of not drawing undue attention to ourselves by what we wear or how we act. However, such a definition doesn't capture the full meaning. For one, modesty isn't just a negative command, and being modest doesn't imply a lack of care about appearance. Quite the opposite! Modesty is actually a positive and active approach whereby we seek to respect others and draw attention to God through our words and way of life.[46]

But in America, Christians have adopted a kind of false modesty in our evangelism. We never presume to suggest that we're actually holier than someone else. Furthermore, we think our gospel is more credible to others when they see us as mostly like them. We've come to believe that God is most glorified and people are most evangelized when the church is either hip and trendy or when it's struggling and broken and weak.[47] So the last thing we'd want to do is portray ourselves as either holy or healthy—and most certainly not better than anyone else.

Our great danger isn't being like the pious Jews in Jesus's day, doing external acts of worship to receive the approval and admiration of others. Instead, the threat to the American church is the opposite, though equally sinister, form of hypocrisy. We want to be inwardly transformed without showing any outward change. We don't want to stand out. It's as if we've lit a candle but are trying our best to hide it under

---

46 Modesty is a taboo topic in American Christianity, but I'm convinced it's a critical consideration related to our evangelism.

47 This idea might originate from Paul's words about the treasured light of Christ being in jars of clay. However, the brokenness and weakness Paul referred to was his physical suffering, not an ongoing struggle with sin or moral inferiority.

a basket. But the whole point of a lit lamp is that others will see it (Matt. 5:15).

DIFFERENT FOR A REASON

Christians aren't just different for the sake of being different. The goal of our evident love and godliness is that others will recognize our good deeds—even ones they currently think are evil—and glorify the Father at the day of Christ's return (2:12).[48] Our lives are different for a reason: to be a window display to God's nature, with the dual purpose of their salvation and God's greater glory.

Peter challenges his readers to not be conformed to the passions of their former ignorance (1:14), to make a clean break with the futile ways of their forefathers (1:18), to put away slander and envy and deceit (2:1), to abstain from fleshly cravings (2:11), and to leave behind their old lifestyle of drunkenness, sensuality, and debauchery (4:3). Instead, they are to demonstrate self-control, live with a good conscience, bless others with love, walk in holiness, and keep their conduct honorable.

But living this way comes at a cost, especially when we're outcasts. For one, Peter suggests that his readers could face real suffering and harm even for doing good (3:13–14). Add to that the pressure of constant mocking, which could easily

---

48 It's not completely clear if Peter understood they would become believers through observing the good conduct of Christians. However, those who ultimately glorify God seem to be those who repent and believe (Rev. 11:13; 16:9). Calvin took Peter's words to imply salvation, assuming that "the unbelieving, led by our good works, would become obedient to God, and thus by their own conversion give glory to him." Calvin, *Commentaries on the Catholic Epistles* (Grand Rapids: Eerdmans, 1948), 79. A good number of modern commentators also take this view.

tempt them to conform to those around them.

Here we should recognize that the experience of exile isn't always one where we have traditional enemies who draw lines and fight battles. They don't merely shun and exclude. Sometimes—or even more frequently—exile looks like good friends who want to include us in their fun. But when you don't go along with their wickedness, they scoff and deride you for not participating in their sin (4:4).

This derision can occur when you decline the invitation to your friend's bachelor party. When you refuse unethical business practices. When you turn down the offer of drugs. When you won't cheat on the test. When you abstain from mocking political leaders. When you don't sleep around. When you excuse yourself from an inappropriate movie. When you won't lie about your age. When you don't laugh at crass humor. When you refuse to break the law. When you won't join in endless gossip. When you miss the Sunday soccer game.

When we do any of those things and more—when we're visibly *other*—the pain of ridicule and social exclusion can be sharp. Unless we're willing to be different and face the consequences, we'll never make those hard decisions. But if we're never different, how will people ever be convinced of the gospel and respond by glorifying God?

Peter knew that one of the greatest dangers for exiles is the constant feeling of being *other*. As a result, they can bow to social pressure, causing them to lose their unique identity as distinct from others. Often as Christians we think that by adapting to our surroundings we'll mitigate the forces against us. If we cave on this or that issue, maybe they won't ridicule us as much at work or in school. In fact, we may even believe that the more we behave like them the better the chances they'll accept us and our gospel. We can somehow buy into the lie that Christianity will be more appealing the more it looks like the world.

But to be an exile—to be *other*—is central to the Christian calling. We're strangers in our land. And that's good news. Sometimes the experience of exile can actually remind us of our true identity and home. I know I've experienced this reminder as an expat living abroad. In fact, anthropologists have observed that immigrants and refugees sometimes have a greater love for their national identity and a greater commitment to cultural preservation than those who remain in the homeland. That's because when you have everything stripped away, you cling to what makes you who you are. We too, as we experience increased isolation and shame in our country of origin, have an opportunity to embrace the foreignness that comes with being like God and a citizen of his kingdom.

Daniel was a Jewish man taken captive from Jerusalem to serve in the royal court of King Nebuchadnezzar in Babylon. There, Daniel's captors tried to force assimilation on him and the other deportees, integrating them into the Babylonian culture by changing their names, status, and diet. But Daniel was committed to maintaining a distinction wherever possible.

Rather than defile himself with the food and drink of the Babylonians, he resolved to maintain his purity by denying himself his allotted portion from the king's table. Such a bold move was surely filled with risk and disgrace. It also meant forsaking the finer things of Babylon. While Daniel could have chosen a more silent protest, his resistance was designed to demonstrate to his superiors the benefit of his diet under the blessing of his God. At the end of 10 days, he wanted them to carefully observe his appearance and deal with him "according to what you see" (Dan. 1:13).

Throughout the book of Daniel we encounter that consistent willingness to maintain a noticeable distinction, even at a cost. His friends, when commanded to bow down to the golden image, refused to kneel. Instead they took a stand, figuratively and literally, visible to their opponents. And Daniel, a man with whom his enemies could find no fault, on learning that prayer had been outlawed, went home, threw open the windows, and proceeded to pray as he always had three times a day.[49]

As those in exile, Daniel and his friends repeatedly looked for ways to preserve their religious convictions and cultural distinction. They generally managed to do so with respect for their authorities and also with a bold testimony. They even sustained a good reputation as citizens and servants of the Babylonian kingdom. But they were also willing to openly be different, even committing civil disobedience, as a way to demonstrate their true allegiance and personal holiness.

Today, as a Christian assembly of exiles, we don't need to become more like the world in an attempt to win their approval or affection. Instead, we should celebrate our

---

49 Jesus condemned praying to be seen by others (Matt. 6:5), but Daniel's action wasn't motivated by pious hypocrisy.

uniqueness. We should embrace being different. We should even desire, like Daniel, to have our "set-apartness" become more and more visible, to have our love and good deeds become unavoidable, to have our holiness be so evident that people—who this very day hate Christianity—would have to take account of what they see.

We're likely still many decades from severe persecution in this land, but there may come a day when Christian worship becomes completely alien and immoral. It might even reach the point of becoming illegal. But the trials of those days will also be an occasion for the gospel, because they'll present an incredible opportunity to be holy and *to be like God*. As Peter wrote, "If when you do good and suffer for it you endure, this is a gracious thing in the sight of God. For to this you have been called, because Christ also suffered for you, leaving you an example, so that you might follow in his steps" (2:20–21).

DOING GOOD TO BE SEEN BY GOD — AND HEARD

The mere thought of physical persecution might be difficult for us to even consider. However, I don't find that passage as hard to swallow as Peter's instructions to husbands. For me, it's one of the most challenging verses in all the Bible:

> Husbands, live with your wives in an understanding way, showing honor to the woman as the weaker vessel, since they are heirs with you of the grace of life, so that your prayers may not be hindered. (3:8)

On the surface, the sense of this verse is fairly plain.

Husbands are to live with humility and grace toward their wives, recognizing the fragility of their humanity and the glory of their eternal inheritance. It's a beautiful thought, really— until you come to grips with the final phrase: so your prayers aren't hindered.

One of the most difficult lessons of my life came while living in Central Asia and watching my wife suffer physically. Her health deteriorated before my eyes. We saw doctors in and out of the country. She took tests and waited for results. Then she took more tests. Eventually the doctors' answers made it clear they didn't have answers, so we quit anticipating results, and she quit taking their tests.

But right in the middle of all of her suffering, the ugliness and cruelty of my own selfishness became a cancer in my heart. On many occasions I spoke with frustration to her. I could get annoyed at her lack of contribution to our parenting. I would be bothered by her occasional inability to help around the home or in ministry. At times I became irritated whenever she woke me at midnight in distress. Her illness was inconveniencing me, and I couldn't be troubled with her pain.

It honestly hurts to write those words, for they reveal much that was wrong with my priorities. I wanted to reach others for Christ, but I didn't always want to care for my wife. I wanted to excel in language study and focus on sermon preparation; I didn't want to go to the doctor. We needed to have believers in our home for Bible study; I needed her to get the house ready. On multiple occasions, sometimes for extended seasons, I was most definitely not living with her in an understanding way, showing honor in view of her weakness and glory. As a result, I have no doubt that many of my sincerest prayers for ministry were left unheard and unanswered.

Peter uses this reality, the negative motivation of unanswered prayer, as a subtle warning to men. He challenges husbands to live in compassionate understanding so their prayers wouldn't be hindered—because we don't just live godly lives to be seen by others. We live *coram deo*—before God. He is watching. Though as we learn here, if we continue in sin, he won't always listen.

Do you have categories for that God? Or have you been taught that because of his unconditional love, he never deals with us according to our sin?

That's not the way Peter understood the Christian life. In fact, he repeatedly highlights this particular truth about prayer— what God hears from us depends on what he sees in us. So Peter could write that if you're going to call on the Father, who judges according to people's deeds, then you need to take care how you conduct your lives (1:17). He could quote from Psalm 34 to establish that God is observing our actions, and his ears are open to the prayers of the righteous (3:12). He could also call believers tempted to fall back into sin to be self-controlled and sober-minded for the sake of their prayers (4:7). And, of course, he could tell inconsiderate husbands like me that we can go ahead and forget having him answer our cries for help until we get our hearts in order.[50]

---

50 The Old Testament teaches that God answers the prayers of the righteous and not the wicked (Ps. 34:15; 145:18; Isa. 1:5; 58:3; 59:2; Mic. 3:4). The concept appears less frequently in the New Testament, though it's especially present in 1 Peter (James 5:16; cf. John 9:31).

I'm sure you can see how this truth matters for our everyday lives. So many frustrated Christians describe their prayer experience as dead and cold. They don't know if their prayers are even making it past the ceiling. Usually in such situations, our go-to answer is to affirm that God hears and answers all their prayers. Maybe his answer for now is to wait, but he's listening. However, I wonder if our confidence is misplaced, and I wonder if their sense of God's deafness is sometimes more accurate than we realize. Could it be that their unconfessed sin has hindered their prayers?

Of course, you can also see how this influences our attempts at evangelism. We likely all have unbelieving friends and family whom we love and care for, whom we pray for regularly. We plead with God for their salvation, for their eyes to be opened to see the light of God's glory in the face of Christ (2 Cor. 4:6). But how often are those prayers short-circuited by our lack of purity, by harsh words, by lustful glances, or by proud thoughts?

God isn't just concerned with our evangelism, as if that's the most important aspect of the Christian life. One of my concerns in writing a book on evangelism is that you could come away with the sense that our lives should totally revolve around reaching others—that witnessing is our singular purpose. But it's not.

Of course, God is concerned with the salvation of sinners. But he's also deeply concerned with your holiness. And all of that because his ultimate concern is for his own glory.

While I spent many days bothered by my wife's physical ailments and weakness, thinking she was hindering the work of the ministry, the reality was that my inconsiderate self-interest and lack of understanding was more of a hindrance to God's mission in our city. I'm convinced it was the reason for unanswered prayers. In truth, I had everything backward. God was using her evident hope through suffering and her visible holiness before others to be a light to our neighbors, even as she lay helpless on the floor of Asmin's apartment.

Our conduct is critical to our witness as exiles. We must remember that our neighbors are watching. Like Asmin, they all know if our walk matches our talk. Our extended family, friends, coworkers, and children can all see if our faith is real. And one way God has ordained for them to be drawn to Christ is through the visible, observable testimony of our holiness. They need to see we're different, that we're like our Father, and that our deeds are good. Only then, as we shine before others, will some of them actually see the light.

CHAPTER 6

THE

GOOD

NEWS OF

HOME

"ABOVE ALL, KEEP LOVING ONE ANOTHER EARNESTLY, SINCE LOVE COVERS A MULTITUDE OF SINS. SHOW HOSPITALITY TO ONE ANOTHER WITHOUT GRUMBLING. AS EACH HAS RECEIVED A GIFT, USE IT TO SERVE ONE ANOTHER, AS GOOD STEWARDS OF GOD'S VARIED GRACE."

—PETER THE APOSTLE (1 PET. 4:8-10)

I leaned forward on the edge of the cushioned armchair, prayerful and unnerved. My palms were clammy, my lungs heavy. On the table next to me sat my Bible. In its front cover I had tucked a letter for Hira.

Hira was the middle-aged and single mother of Meryem, the teenaged girl we had met six months previous. Now both of them were in the kitchen with my wife while I waited impatiently in the living room. Our families had just finished a meal together, but next came our usual after-dinner conversation—a conversation I was dreading.

Since our first encounter with Meryem, we had made it our purpose to befriend Hira. Over the course of those months our relationship with both of them grew through regular hospitality. Nearly every week they would come to our home for dinner or dessert. Or we would go to theirs. Inevitably, either at the table or on the floor afterward, we would enter into a lively debate about Christianity.

Hira had strong convictions about Islam. She was also concerned, not surprisingly, by the influence we were having on her daughter. However, our disagreements didn't keep us apart. Over the course of time—and over a lot of good food—we became genuine friends. Hira was incredibly gracious to us and felt a special kinship with my wife. They shared the same birth year. They shared many of the same health issues. And now, in a way, they both shared the same daughter.

Meryem had recently come to faith in Christ and already started to view us as an extension of her family. Now she was ready to be baptized. Hira, however, was slower to believe. She was still unconvinced by the gospel and remained skeptical of the Jesus we proclaimed.

When Hira came in from the kitchen, she sat down across the table from me. Her breathing was uneven. I slowly took the paper from my Bible, unfolded it, and asked her to read the prepared agreement. Since her daughter was a minor, we were asking for parental consent, including her signature, to baptize Meryem. This was our way of honoring Hira, so I candidly reiterated our terms: "We will not do this without your permission." As the words exited my mouth, I prepared for the worst.

But then, almost without hesitation, she signed it. She even agreed to be at her daughter's side that Easter weekend. In fact, immediately following the baptism—before Meryem's hair even had time to dry—I witnessed Hira do something she never had before. She walked into the living room, settled into a comfortable chair, and picked up a Bible. She then began to read.

HOSPITALITY FOR THE SAKE OF THE GOSPEL

Hospitality isn't a primary theme in the book of 1 Peter, certainly not on level with exile and suffering or hope and holiness. But it does figure prominently in one important passage.

As Peter begins to wrap up his instructions to first-century believers, he writes that "above all" they should love one another (4:8). Love was to be the crown jewel of their transformed lives. However, love wasn't simply the highest of all commands, it was behind and before every other instruction in the letter: to be humble and respect others, to not slander or revile, to walk in holiness, and to declare God's praises. That's because all Christian law is encapsulated in this one command—love.

But it's especially interesting how Peter fills out his climactic call to love. After stating its preeminence, he gives one specific example of how they should express this love: show hospitality (4:9). Peter sandwiches the command to gracious hospitality between the twin admonitions to love and service. It's as if being hospitable is one primary way he envisioned they would, through love, serve one another.

Hospitality was crucial for mission in the early church. Ambassadors of the gospel would travel from town to town with little provision. They depended on the generous welcome of local believers for room and board, to sustain them and later send them on their way. Homes were also the gathering place of early assemblies. Churches relied on members opening their homes for regular meetings and worship.[51]

Such regular hospitality no doubt took a toll on Christians. While their culture and living conditions were clearly different from ours, their temptations were the same. Continuously having others in their homes was tiring and taxing. It cost financially. It took time. So Peter added that making space for such repeated interruption and inconvenience should be done without grumbling. They were to love one another cheerfully, giving of their most valuable resources—even their homes—for the sake of Christ.

Of course, that kind of glad generosity was directed primarily to believers. So what does hospitality have to do with evangelism?

For one, we'd be mistaken to assume that Peter limited such kindness to only brothers and sisters in Christ. Our homes and our tables aren't reserved for people like us. As Jesus said, our love and greeting should also be for those different from us (Matt. 5:47). The Christian call to hospitality includes a love for outsiders—for strangers, foreigners, and the *other*.[52] It implies sharing our homes with sinners. As such, the ministry of hospitality is essential for our evangelistic endeavor.

---

51 Thomas R. Schreiner, *1, 2 Peter, Jude*, New American Commentary (Nashville, B&H: 2003), 213.

52 The Greek word for hospitality (*philozenia*) comes from a compound of "love" and "stranger."

That was definitely our family's experience in Central Asia. We didn't have the opportunity for large outreach events. Cold-call evangelism wasn't a viable option. And we couldn't count solely on visitors coming to church. So in the case of Hira and many others like her, we employed hospitality for the sake of the gospel. We regularly invited Muslim friends and neighbors into our home for a meal. If they weren't comfortable eating at our house (perhaps for religious reasons), we'd go to theirs. We'd also meet them at a restaurant or café. And speaking as someone who loves to eat, I can honestly say it made for a great evangelistic strategy!

The story of Matthew represents a perfect example of what this can look like. Shortly after his call to follow Jesus, Matthew opened up his home to friends and former colleagues. Luke records that he hosted a great feast, so this wasn't a spontaneous or random occurrence, but one that took preparation. It came at expense. And it revealed an intentionality to introduce his friends to the Savior. We learn this by Jesus's own admission. He wasn't at the party just to hang out and have a good time. Rather, his purpose for being there was to call sinners to repentance (Luke 5:27–32).

INVITATION TO THE TABLE

The all-American proverb from *Field of Dreams*, "If you build it, they will come," has characterized the Western approach to evangelism and church growth for some generations. We have a long history of promoting large crusades or tent revivals that draw a crowd for a gospel presentation. In fact, many Christians are explicitly taught or implicitly assume that inviting their neighbor to such an event amounts to evangelism. But what they're really doing is counting on someone else to preach the gospel and counting on others to actually want to attend.

Still today, many churches seek to do outreach primarily by bringing people in. They practice an attractional model of mission. As a result, our greatest aspirations in evangelism have often been that our neighbors would come with us to church, send their kids to VBS, or attend a Christian camp or concert. But we need to recognize that the greatest hope for our unbelieving neighbors isn't them coming to us, but God sending us to them. It's us living on mission in their neighborhoods, and our home becoming a place where they can meet the Savior.

I'm not necessarily advocating for a moratorium on invitations—I just think the venue needs to change. We need to start inviting people to our own tables.

Last year I listened to an NPR interview with a researcher from the University of Chicago. She was studying the effects of sharing a meal when negotiating a business transaction. Over the course of the study, she found that those who ate together—specifically, who ate the same foods—were more likely to come to a settlement faster. While the research didn't reveal a definitive cause, her findings suggested a strong link between the experience of a shared meal and arriving at a mutual agreement.

Of course, I'm not suggesting that the secret to effective evangelism is eating the same food as someone else. But there's an undeniable human connection that happens when we break bread with others. Sharing a meal communicates humility and respect. It demonstrates tangible love and service. A common meal has a way of opening doors for communication and fostering genuine understanding. Often—at least when the food and drink is good—there's also an experience of shared joy.

As such, I believe inviting others to our own tables can be an important first step to an effective evangelistic strategy. People who would never cross the threshold of a church will still walk through your front door. People who are indifferent to religion or disinclined to Christianity will still appreciate a friendly dinner invitation. They'll gladly accept a free meal and, in the process, may just listen to you rejoice in free forgiveness.

In his Gospel account, Matthew records twice in short succession that Jesus reclined at table with sinners—this after promising that many would join at his table in the kingdom of heaven (Matt. 9:10; 8:11). It's as if Matthew understood the two actions to be connected. One way sinners enter the kingdom is by first entering our kitchen. Some will only come to the table of the Lord after first coming to our dinner table.

The reality is, as we face increasing exile in our land, we'll need to rediscover the necessity of hospitality for the gospel. Church attendance will likely continue to wane, and with it pulpit evangelism. Meanwhile, Christian witness could be all but silenced in the workplace or the classroom. Public spaces could suddenly become "safe," off-limits to proselytizing or any religious conversation. But our private homes will long remain a haven for free speech, the perfect place for reasoning with others about the gospel.

We'll want to leverage that opportunity by continuously opening our doors to others, especially to people unlike us. To Latino, Caucasian, or African American households. To poor widows or the unemployed. To Hindus and atheists. To international students. To migrant workers. To a wealthy businessperson. To a gay couple. To sinners of every sex, stripe, and status.

HOLINESS IS NOT THE ENEMY OF HOSPITALITY

Having read the last chapter, you might assume I'm advocating for a set-apart lifestyle that *physically* separates us from sinners. That to be holy requires us to completely remove ourselves from the presence of evil—even the appearance of it.[53] But that would be a reconstruction of the faulty law-fencing of the Pharisees.

In the story of Matthew's dinner party, we learn that some Pharisees were scandalized by Jesus's presence at the party. The disreputable nature of Matthew's former job, along with his unsavory guests, appalled the Pharisees. They were dismayed that Jesus would choose to eat and drink with tax-collectors and sinners. They couldn't reconcile their concept of holiness with Jesus's commitment to love.

But purity and love aren't mutually exclusive. Actually, Peter

---

[53] Some would base this on their reading or translation of 1 Thess. 5:22, but I find it contradictory to Jesus's example. As Luke records, Jesus admitted that he came eating and drinking, a friend to swindling tax collectors and irreligious sinners. This behavior made him appear to some to be "a glutton and a drunkard" (Luke 7:34). But their misperceptions didn't stop Jesus from continuing his pattern of associating with sinners, even letting a "woman of the city" touch his feet in the immediately following pericope (Luke 7:36–39; see also Luke 5:30; 15:2; Matt. 9:11).

self-consciously puts the two together in his first epistle. He writes that believers had obeyed the gospel and been purified in order to love. Therefore, they were to show genuine and earnest love to others from a pure heart (2:22). Peter's repeated emphasis on "set-apartness" was not in opposition to a generous compassion. It was an expression of it. In other words, their call to holiness was never meant to be the enemy of hospitality (see also Matt. 5:47–48).

We find the same lesson in the story of the Good Samaritan. In Luke 10, Jesus affirms that the summary of the law was love for God and neighbor. Then, similar to Peter, he colors in the picture of neighbor-love with a depiction of hospitality. You likely know the account.

A traveler from Jerusalem was ambushed, robbed, and left for dead. A priest came by and saw the man, but avoided him. A Levite did the same (both likely hesitant to defile themselves with a corpse or have a run-in with robbers). But then a Samaritan approached and did the unexpected. He stopped and helped the half-dead Jew. He showed love and generosity, caring for all his needs. Whereas the religious Jews were unable to demonstrate mercy, the "ungodly" Samaritan represented true love of neighbor—and true law keeping—through his sacrificial hospitality to a total stranger.

In this story we encounter both great danger and also opportunity. The danger is for those who seek to protect their holiness by keeping sinners at a distance, those who try to remain clean without having compassion. As we face social exclusion, the temptation will be to push others away. Victims easily become victimizers. The hurt have a way of hurting others. The danger is for holy exiles to make everyone who's not like them also an outcast—of becoming an exclusive people by creating our own restrictive circles.

But it need not be so. The Samaritan was a social castaway, despised by the Jews. Yet in Jesus's story he was the one who knew how to show genuine love and hospitality. That's because when you suffer as an outsider you have the capacity to empathize with the hurting, show compassion for the suffering, and offer kindness to sinners. You understand the value of honor and a home, because yours has been taken away. This, as you might guess, was particularly true of the oppressed African American slaves nearly two centuries ago.

James Redpath, a reporter working for the *New-York Tribune* in the mid-1800s, recounted his experience of Negro hospitality while traveling through the antebellum South. One night on his journey through the Carolinas, he was lost and alone. A storm was nearing. Clouds of ink blotted out the moon and stars. Hearing a rumble in the distance, he sought shelter in a nearby plantation. But when he inquired about emergency lodging he was refused, even after much pleading.

Redpath eventually relented and went his way, walking down some railroad tracks hoping to find another option. When he couldn't, he returned to the original homestead. Again he appealed to the master of the house, but to no avail. Finally, as rain began to pour down, he spotted a small "negro hut" in the distant woods. He ran for cover and was welcomed—though with some suspicion—by a group of slaves. That night they made room for him in their crowded shack.

Reflecting on that experience and his collective observations from extensive travels in the South, Redpath wrote:

> I did not see any of that celebrated hospitality for which Southerners are perpetually praising themselves. They are very hospitable to strangers who come to them well introduced—who don't need hospitality, in fact; but they are very much the reverse when a stranger presents himself under other and unfavorable circumstances. The richer class of planters are especially inhospitable. *The negroes are the hospitable class of the South.*[54]

Sadly, many of those white "planters," as Redpath called them, were likely self-professed Christians. And while we may not be guilty of their overt racism, our attempts at hospitality can still mimic theirs. We might show generous hospitality, but only to people like us—never to those of a different race or background, a different belief or persuasion, or a different social class. We welcome others into our home, but generally those who don't even need it. Our hospitality is only lateral and transactional. We host peers in a system that expects reciprocity, not one that displays free grace.

But real hospitality is like that of the Negro slaves. It doesn't require limitless resources or a luxury kitchen with an open floor plan. The only requirement of hospitality is love. Love that serves others rather than serving ourselves. Love that seeks to use our home and our resources, like Matthew, to introduce people to Jesus. But sadly what we often label as hospitality is merely entertaining—it's just more of that old Southern hospitality, dignified and genteel, but knowing nothing of sacrifice or incongruity.

---

54 From James Redpath's *The Roving Editor*, 1859, 139 (emphasis mine).

If we're going to make a difference for the gospel with our homes, we'll need to see our homes and tables as an extension of the kingdom—where there's always "plenty good room." But that will mean our hospitality will need to be visibly different from the world's. Or to put it another way, our love will need to be holy.[55]

HOSPITALITY IS PART OF THE GOSPEL

If you ever visited Asma's apartment, you would instantly know something was wrong. Upon opening the front door, even before entering, the smell of mildew would greet you. Once inside, you'd notice her belongings and textbooks covered in mold. Her home was dark, dank, and probably unsafe to occupy. But she couldn't afford any better. As it was, she often needed help from us just to keep the heat on.

Asma was a young Central Asian believer in significant financial trouble. Her parents, becoming suspicious of her conversion, had withdrawn their financial support. She could no longer pay for school, so she dropped out of college halfway through. In the first year we knew her, she was able to find employment at a home goods store. But even working endless days and weekends, she couldn't make a livable wage.

The following summer, Asma was desperate for a break from work. She also wanted out of her damp apartment. So she decided to visit family. Having scraped together enough

---

55 Rosaria Butterfield's *The Gospel Comes with a House Key* (Wheaton, IL: Crossway, 2018) provides a good introduction to neighbor-love through hospitality.

money to buy a ticket, she took the 12-hour bus ride home—only to never return.

What exactly happened when she reunited with family was hard to ascertain. For one, her availability to talk on the phone or social media was severely limited. Her parents had confiscated her belongings. They told her they wouldn't allow her to return to the city where she had Christian friends. In the end, they basically held her hostage in her own house.

In fact, a full two years passed before Asma was able to come back, still without her parents' blessing, to our former city. She managed to re-enroll in the local university, but she was still struggling financially. The challenge of taking a full course load and providing for her needs continued to weigh heavily.

Knowing of her constant struggles, I reached out to check in on her situation and let Asma know of our prayers. She messaged back to say that her parents continued to be angry. Her father was still refusing to help with her living expenses. But she reported with thanksgiving that a believing Canadian family had provided their home as a place to stay, one that was clean and safe.

As I prepared to sign off, I wrote, "Your brothers and sisters in America love you." To which Asma quickly replied, "I'm so happy to be a part of this family. I'm just happy to be a stone in this temple." Then she added, "I love you, my family, very much."

What you quickly realize living in a Muslim nation, where Christians are an extreme minority, is that hospitality isn't just a method of evangelism. Hospitality often becomes part of the gospel offer.

For people to turn from their birth family and inherited faith to follow Christ is to embrace a life-long experience of exile. They face social persecution. Their families disown them. They can lose their place at school, their job, their spouse, and even their children. They may, quite literally, be kicked to the curb. So when you present the gospel to them, you have to be ready to offer a place to stay.

In fact, I know of at least one church in the country where we lived that reserved rooms in their sanctuary for this purpose. If someone expressed interest in following Christ and being baptized, the congregation was prepared to put them up for a time. If their relatives became incensed or violent, or if they disowned them, the new believers would have an immediate place of refuge.

You might see how providing temporary housing could be helpful or even necessary in certain contexts, but not in America. However, I'm convinced it will be in days ahead. As family and friends react in anger at their loved ones' conversion. As becoming a Christian means stepping away from a partner and a house, an occupation and income, or leaving a whole community. As new followers of Christ walk into immediate exile. In such situations, the church will need to provide the family and home that the gospel promises.

REWARD OF HOUSES AND FAMILY

In Mark 3:21 there's a strange, isolated account reporting that

Jesus's family "went out to seize him, for they were saying, 'He is out of his mind.'" Suddenly, in the next paragraph, the narrative spotlight shifts to the scribes from Jerusalem. They came down to Capernaum and accused Jesus of being possessed by Beelzebul. The Jewish leaders attributed his power and miracles to Satan! Then, at the end of their exchange, the story again returns to Jesus's relatives. We encounter them standing outside of the home in Capernaum, calling out to Jesus.

Their summons was an attempt to stop him. Jesus's family truly thought he had gone mad. Their assessment of his ministry was basically in line with that of the scribes, so they were taking action. They wanted Jesus to drop his crowd-creating shtick. It was time to come home. The show was over.

But when Jesus learned of Mary and her sons calling out for him, his curt response was striking: "Who are my mother and my brothers?" (Mark 3:34).

Jesus was abandoned and forsaken by the most important people in his life, not just by Roman rulers and godless magistrates. He was condemned by Judaism's elite, by the religious authorities and scholars of his day. We can easily miss these enormous consequences, but to cross the cultural gatekeepers in a tightly guarded religious system was to mark yourself as an outlier and a heretic. It meant incredible personal shame. Perhaps more significantly, especially in Middle Eastern society, it simultaneously meant unbearable reproach on the family name. So even Mary and her other sons turned against him.[56]

As a result, Jesus faced exile on almost every level, both emotional and also physical. He was completely rejected and ostracized. But in the middle of such social exclusion Jesus found his belonging in a family greater than his blood relatives. Because, as Jesus said, "Whoever does the will of God, he is my brother and sister and mother" (Mark 3:35). His true clan was the larger gathering, the great host of heaven, all who belonged to his Father. And so it is for us, his followers.

Later on in Mark's Gospel[57] we come to a parallel experience in the life of the disciples when they encountered a rich young man. Jesus challenged the man to go and sell all that he had. In response, Peter—the same Peter who later wrote his epistle to Asian exiles—felt the need to bring to his Lord's attention that he, along with all the other disciples, had already left everything to follow him.

And here Jesus's words are of immeasurable weight and inestimable value for believers suffering today in exile for the gospel:

> Jesus said, "Truly, I say to you, there is no one who has left house or brothers or sisters or mother or father or

---

56 At this point in time, Jesus's family seems to have turned against him. According to John 7:5, Jesus's brothers didn't believe in him or understand his mission. However, later biblical accounts would suggest that they came to trust and follow him (Acts 1:14). For more detailed discussion on the translation and a defense of this interpretation of Mark 3:21, see France, *The Gospel of Mark* (Grand Rapids, Eerdmans: 2002), 165–67.

57 Church tradition has historically seen Peter behind Mark's Gospel. The early Church Father Papias, writing around A.D. 130, attests to Mark becoming "Peter's interpreter" and writing with accuracy what he remembered (Eusebius, *Ecclesiastical History*, 3.39.15).

children or lands, for my sake and for the gospel, who will not receive a hundredfold now in this time, houses and brothers and sisters and mothers and children and lands, with persecutions, and in the age to come eternal life." (Mark 10:29–30)

Do you see it? The reward of the gospel includes houses and families! Jesus left his heavenly home only to be forsaken by his earthly family and by Jewish authorities. The Son of Man didn't even have a place to lay his head (Luke 9:58). But in his experience of exile and through his cross, Jesus inherited a family and a home. And here, for his beleaguered disciples, he promised the same. They had left houses and brothers and lands and fathers for his name's sake. In return, they could expect the same and much more.

This is the good news of home for displaced followers of Jesus. Christian hospitality isn't just what we do to show kindness to strangers or unbelievers. It's certainly not what we do to entertain guests or show off our home. Christian hospitality can't even be reduced to a sacrificial act of generosity and love, because in reality it's far more. Christian hospitality is the reward of the gospel. It's a foretaste in this life of a shared inheritance in the next. It's a seat at the table now, the shadow of a future feast where we'll recline at table in the kingdom.

It's for Asma, a forsaken and impoverished young woman in Central Asia, who has left everything to follow Jesus, having lost her home, her father, and maybe a big portion of her future. But who, in so doing, has gained countless siblings in Christ. She has a family in America who loves and prays for her. She also has a home thanks to a Canadian brother and sister. And she has a cloud of witnesses cheering her on.

HONOR AND HOME

One of my favorite Bible stories as a child comes from 2 Samuel. I can still remember my father teaching about Mephibosheth, the young boy who had an unfortunate fall, a tragic accident that left him crippled on the fateful day his father and grandfather, King Saul, were killed (2 Sam. 4:4). But like any good story, it didn't end there. Years later Mephibosheth experienced an unexpected rise to honor in the house of David (2 Sam. 9).

Normally in the ancient world when a king ascended to the throne, he wiped out all the competition, specifically any descendants from a rival dynasty. But when David became king, he did the opposite. Years earlier he had made a covenant with Jonathan, the father of Mephibosheth, that he would do good to his offspring. It was a strategically hazardous promise at the time, knowing that whoever survived in Saul's family would present a credible threat to his reign.

Shortly after rising to power, David inquired of the state of Saul's line. When he discovered that Saul still had a living descendant, he immediately called Mephibosheth into his presence. David was resolved to keep his covenant with Jonathan and show kindness to his son. So he did, restoring all of Saul's land to the family, providing work for his servants, and granting Mephibosheth a permanent seat at the king's table.[58]

---

58 David described God as "Father of the fatherless" who "settles the solitary in a home" (Ps. 68:5–6). So by bringing Mephibosheth into his home, David was being like God (Ps. 113:6–8). For a more extended meditation on the story of Mephibosheth, see Jayson Georges and Mark D. Baker, *Ministering in Honor-Shame Cultures: Biblical Foundations and Practical Essentials* (Downers Grove, IL: IVP Academic, 2016), 83–86.

David took the person who should have been his greatest enemy and made him a close companion. He took an individual disgraced by disability and exalted him to a place of honor. He rescued a man destined to live out his days in hiding or political exile and gave him a home, even a seat at his own table. And, of course, in so doing King David was just like—and pointed to—King Jesus.

Jesus loved us while we were still his enemies. He transformed us from rebels into friends. Those who were not a people he made his own people (2:10). He brought us into his kingdom, and we have been adopted into the royal family, given a place at the table and a share in his inheritance.[59] In his Father's house there are many rooms, because Jesus is preparing a place for us (John 14:2).

As we've seen from the letter of 1 Peter, to follow in the footsteps of a crucified king is to walk into exile, into shame and social exclusion, and even persecution. But the gospel of Jesus, as genuine good news, simultaneously welcomes us into honor and a home. That is the hope of future glory. It's the hope that began this book and now ends it. Hospitality is one way of tangibly experiencing the good news of home in the here and now. It's having a table prepared for us in the presence of our enemies.

---

59 The end-time vision in Isa. 25:6–8 is of a great feast prepared by the Lord for his people where he will remove their shame and reproach from all the earth.

CONCLUSION

"HUMBLE YOURSELVES, THEREFORE,
UNDER THE MIGHTY HAND OF GOD
SO THAT AT THE PROPER TIME HE
MAY EXALT YOU, . . . AND AFTER
YOU HAVE SUFFERED A LITTLE
WHILE, THE GOD OF ALL GRACE,
WHO HAS CALLED YOU TO HIS
ETERNAL GLORY IN CHRIST, WILL
HIMSELF RESTORE, CONFIRM,
STRENGTHEN, AND ESTABLISH
YOU. TO HIM BE THE DOMINION
FOREVER AND EVER. AMEN."

—PETER THE APOSTLE (1 PET. 5:6, 10-11)

If you've made it this far—and if you picked up this book in the first place—it's likely because you desire to grow in personal evangelism. You probably sense, as I do for myself, that you're coming up short in your responsibility to make Christ known. As a result, you may bear the burden of failure. Perhaps you're simultaneously disheartened with the church's attempts to reach the lost in our communities. But that's not too surprising. My guess is that all of us feel some measure of discontentment when it comes to our pursuit of evangelism, whether individually or corporately.

But I've also observed a growing anxiety in American Christianity about our changing place in the world. There's a rolling undercurrent of fear and unease about what the future will hold for us as believers in Jesus. Leaders in various spheres of our culture seem to be conspiring against Christ and his church, threatening our way of life. So we wonder what our experience will be as a shrinking minority. And that's not all. We also wonder how we'll accomplish our mission without the status and privileges we've come to cherish—and even expect.

So this book has addressed those twin concerns, specifically by positioning the call to evangelism within the context of exile. Taking Peter's first epistle as our guide, we've sought to reorient our thinking and provide a new perspective (which is really an old one) on how to live on mission as strangers in our own land. And now that we've come to the end, my prayer is that you'll put this book down with renewed focus and a big-picture outlook on how to go about this task.

VIEWING ALL OF LIFE AS MISSION

In my experience, many missionaries—even volunteers on short-term ministry trips—tend to consciously approach every moment in relation to mission. They saturate their days with prayer. They consider the intended or unintended consequences of their mannerisms and behavior, being careful how they spend their money, how they dress, and how they interact with others. They demonstrate the utmost respect and honor for locals, even to people drastically different from them. They also view random encounters as God-ordained opportunities, so they purposefully speak with just about anyone—shopkeepers, waiters, and taxi drivers—about their faith.

But somehow when we're in our home country and going about our daily lives, we often lack that self-awareness and mission-focus. We slip into routines. We lose intentionality. This is actually one of the dangers of ministry trips: They can perpetuate our compartmentalized view of mission. Outreach becomes what we do at certain times and places. Evangelism is an event or a program. So we ignore the interconnectedness of witness and daily work. We struggle to live out the truth that effectiveness in evangelism demands both our words and also our way of life.

But this book has tried to marry the extraordinary call to evangelism with the ordinary and the everyday—with how we relate to a spouse who doesn't believe; to neighbors opposed to the Bible; to friends who mock our morality; and even to godless authorities. We've done this by considering how we can embody the tension of simultaneously living in hope and fear, humility and authority, holiness and hospitality. Folded together, these complementary dispositions influence every area of our lives and subsequently every facet of our witness. We've explored how they work concurrently to open up others *to the gospel* while opening our mouths *with the gospel*, helping us remember that we're constantly on mission.

UNDERSTANDING
EXILE AS NORMAL

As I began to think about examples for this book, I was amazed by story after story from Scripture of those who lived as strangers and aliens: people like Abraham and Joseph, Moses and David, Jeremiah and Nehemiah, and of course, Jesus. In fact, Jesus said of his own proverbial experience, "A prophet is not without honor, except in his hometown and among his relatives and in his own household" (Mark 6:4).

Reflecting then on some of these biblical examples in previous chapters has helped to illustrate that exile is the norm for the children of God. It's common in the pages of the Bible, but also across history and throughout the world today. So while my focus has been on a narrow issue (evangelism) for a contemporary audience (American exiles), I've tried to be biblical and global. I've wanted us to hear stories of Central Asians living in a Muslim-majority context and ground the whole book in Peter's epistle to believers in first-century Asia. I've also wanted us to consider how minorities in America are likely to have experience and wisdom for the rest of us on this topic.

In a sense, this isn't just a book about what I believe evangelism needs to become in our unfolding experience of exile in this land; it's about what I believe our evangelism should've been all along—what evangelism could be in any country. It's a biblical argument for how all Christians everywhere should seek to glorify God and reach others in the face of social exclusion. In reality, if we haven't or aren't currently dealing with some level of reproach and shame in this nation, it's likely owing to the fact that we haven't been practicing bold and biblical evangelism in the first place.

CONSIDERING STRANGENESS AS GOOD

Throughout this book I've tried to develop a somewhat subtle theme on the positive potential for our witness *within earthly exile*. As hopes diminish and fears increase, as opponents rise to power and our cultural influence fades, as we become outcasts and even refugees—it's then, at this very moment, that the church will have an incredible opportunity for the gospel.

As I see it, one of the greatest hindrances to everyday evangelism is our desire to fit in and be normal. But exile—coming face to face with the reality that we don't belong—has a way of opening up our horizons to the possibility of being different and strange. We who by nature long to be insiders, to be accepted and approved, can be freed from that burden and as outsiders take the scary step toward being culturally inappropriate—in positive and proactive ways—and do the otherwise unthinkable.

Like Esther, we can open our mouths when it's least expected and when it's risky. Like Daniel, we can look for ways to live with visible distinction and possibly even noncompliance. Like Naaman's servant, we can defy convention and pursue the good of our oppressors. Like the Good Samaritan, we can show unexpected neighbor-love through sacrifice and hospitality. And like Jesus, we can upend social propriety and speak with a disgraced foreigner or dine with a despised sinner.

Being a Christian in America, now more than ever before, puts us on the outside. Personal evangelism relegates us to the fringe. But the fringe isn't always a bad place to be. The voice of outsiders has power because it confronts monotony. A musical note struck off key is the one most easily recognized. Now is not the time for us to try to cohere the Christian message to a shared sensibility, to make the church fit into the surrounding cultural mold. We should keep Christianity weird. And in so doing, we just might reach our neighbors.

SEEING TRIALS (AND EVANGELISM) AS TEMPORARY

One of the primary features of Peter's letter, and one I haven't fully developed, is his value comparison between the temporal and the eternal. Between what is precious and what is passing.

Peter writes that the Christian inheritance is imperishable, undefiled, and unfading (1:4). Trials, on the other hand, only last "for a little while" (1:6). As we endure through momentary suffering, Peter says that our tested faith is purified as through fire; and such faith is more precious than gold that ultimately passes away (1:7). The incomparably precious blood of Christ, however, is imperishable and pure (1:18–19), and the proclaimed gospel is living and abiding. Conversely, Peter reminds us that all flesh—including those who'd oppose us—is like the fading flower of the field (1:23–24).

In those examples we get a glimpse into Peter's comparative analysis on the temporality of suffering, trials, and human opposition in view of eternity. He desires for his readers to feel the full weight of the never-ending, never-diminishing joy and honor they will share with Christ at his return. Peter, as an eyewitness to Jesus's sufferings and his radiant glory (5:1), wants us, as we face numerous trials, to recognize the inestimable and enduring value of the gospel and the hope of heaven. That's why he repeatedly calls us to live in view of the last day (1:5, 7, 13; 2:12; 4:5, 13; 5:4, 6, 10).

As exiles we desperately need this method of appraisal—this other-worldly outlook—to be keenly aware of the shortness of pain and the unrivalled permanence of joy. When our eyes naturally fix on the troubles at hand, we need to zoom out to a wide-angle view, taking in the panorama of eternity to give perspective to our present suffering.

Brothers and sisters, our exile is normal. But the good news is that our shame and earthly sufferings come printed with an expiration date. They'll never outlast or outweigh glory. As a matter of fact, even our evangelism is temporary. So let's be faithful to declare God's praises while it's still called today.